ON ISLAM

JAMES V. SCHALL, S.J.

On Islam

~

A Chronological Record
2002–2018

IGNATIUS PRESS   SAN FRANCISCO

The author wishes to thank the online sites of *Aleteia*, the *Catholic Thing*, *Catholic World Report*, *Crisis*, *Ignatius Insight*, and *MercatorNet*, as well as the *Homiletic and Pastoral Review*, the Fellowship of Catholic Scholars, *Catholic Dossier*, and *Vital Speeches of the Day* for permission to reprint previously published material.

Cover photograph: © Guenter Guni, iStockPhoto.com

Cover design by John Herreid

© 2018 by Ignatius Press, San Francisco
All rights reserved
ISBN 978-1-62164-164-3
Library of Congress Control Number 2017958914
Printed in the United States of America ∞

Contents

Introduction

In philosophical studies, I had a sketchy knowledge of Muslim philosophers. Al-Farabi, Averroës, and Avicenna were frequent names in Aquinas. Indeed, the whole of the *Summa contra gentiles* dealt with the Muslim understanding of Aristotle, Plato, Scripture, and other fundamental writings. It seems ironic, in a way, that the voluntarism that came to rule the Muslim mind is almost identical with the will philosophy that grounds much of Western public life. Voluntarism is the philosophical-theological view that no rational order exists in things or in human nature. What is behind all reality is a will that can always be otherwise. It is not bound to any one truth. The opposite of any position can, with equal right, be valid. Evil can be good; good can be evil, if will, divine or human, not reason, is behind each existing thing. Benedict XVI noted the voluntarism in both Islam and secularism in his Regensburg lecture of September 12, 2006.

But any real awareness of the importance to Europe of Muslim military prowess, however it manifested itself, seemed remote to me decades ago. Christopher Dawson, Bernard Lewis, and Arnold Toynbee, among many others, to be sure, knew of its importance.

In modern times, the real issues in science, philosophy, theology, economics, politics, and literature were, as it seemed, those that occurred within Western civilization itself. It was Europe that had expanded into the rest of the world, including China, India, Africa, and the Americas. The ships of the

European powers, by sailing around southern Africa, simply bypassed the Muslim world, which held the old land routes to the East. The Islamic areas in the past two hundred years or so had been under the rule of the British, the French, the Dutch, the Italians, the Portuguese, or the Russians. The Germans had marked interest and influence in the Middle East and parts of Africa. The Muslims were, for the most part, considered to be backward, fanatical, and in need of complete reform and education in Western, if not Christian, ways. The intellectual issues were those that arose in largely German, English, and French philosophy. Marx dominated most of the latter half of the twentieth century.

In this context, my awareness of Islam as a world force that needed to be reckoned with goes back to my first reading of Hilaire Belloc's 1937 book *The Crusades*. I have never quite forgotten its ending, which was, in effect, that, if Islam ever regained the power it once had, it would continue to do what it did before, expand in the name of Allah.

In the first two centuries after Muhammad, Muslim armies had conquered North Africa, Spain, the Near East, parts of southern Europe, and east to India. What struck me most about Belloc's comment, something that is difficult for people to understand, is his insight that often an idea or a religious movement that once seemed dead can lie dormant for centuries and come back to complete its original mission. From the time of Belloc's book until almost the attacks on the World Trade Center and the Pentagon (2001), the world was concerned with nationalism, Marxism, democracy, and socialism—forces that had their effects also in Islamic areas.

At the time of the September 11, 2001, attacks a number of people remarked on what Belloc wrote in his *Great Heresies*, that less than one hundred years before the American War of Independence a Muslim army was threatening to overrun and destroy Christian civilization. "Vienna . . . was almost taken and was saved only by the Christian army under the command of the King of Poland on a date that ought to be among the most famous in history—September 11, 1683."[1] For those who like this sort of thing, a century earlier, the Isle of Malta sustained a massive attack of Turkish ships ordered by Sultan Suleiman the Magnificent. The famous Knights of Malta under Jean Parisot de la Valette held out, killed the Algerian admiral Dragut, and saw the defeated ships sail away on September 11, 1565.

The 9/11 attacks on American soil were shocking, but what made me especially attentive to what was going on in Islam was something that had happened in Algeria a few years before in a remote mountain monastery inhabited by French Trappist monks. The story has subsequently been made into a poignant French film (*Of Gods and Men* [2010]).

The sheer brutality of the killing of these men was something for which I was not prepared. Since then, we have become almost inured to it by public beheadings of Christians in various Muslim-controlled lands. That anyone can come to a realization of the horror of it all if he but looks is part of the reason why I want to present this chronology of my own reactions and analyses of subsequent events from 2002 to 2018. The husband of a colleague of mine at Georgetown several years ago was the Polish-French writer Laurent Murawiec, who had followed the bloody history of Islam very carefully. It is not my understanding that there is only a bloody history to Islam. It is only that such gore is a part of its history that continues and grows right into our own time.[2]

---

[1] Hilaire Belloc, *The Great Heresies* (San Francisco: Ignatius Press, 2017), 92–93.

[2] William Kilpatrick, "Good Islam vs. Bad Islam", *Crisis Magazine*, May 4, 2016, http://www.crisismagazine.com/2016/good-islam-vs-bad-islam.

Reprinted at the end of this introduction is an article I wrote when I first heard about the murders of the good and innocent monks. This recollection will serve to introduce the subsequent chronology of various events and issues that arose step by step throughout the world as Islam became aware of itself and found new sources of spiritual and jihadist energy. This book is a record of how I have come to look upon Islam as a major factor in current world events. This is not an "anti-Islam" book. In fact, as a political observer, one has to have considerable admiration for the persistent expansion of Islam into our times as well as an awareness of why Westerners do not comprehend its full dynamism and significance.

Basically, I think that Islam is what it says it is, a religion that has an ongoing mission to subject all people to Allah. My basic problem with this mission—a mission grounded in the Qur'an itself—is not its remarkable success and expansion. My problem is its truth. Almost the only place that we can speak of these things today is in a book. Public discussion rarely exists, and academic discussions are seldom better. I make no claim to be an erudite Islamic scholar. But I do think that, with common sense, we can see and judge what an individual or a group does over time. What we end with is an opinion, one that best explains the facts that we see and observe almost every day.

For a number of reasons—from the decline of Christianity in the West, especially as indicated by low birthrates in Europe and America, to the Muslim success in gaining control of enclaves throughout Europe and America—the Muslim future looks very bright. Islamic expansion may be halted or slowed but only temporarily. The city of Tours in the eighth century, and Vienna in the sixteenth, repelled Muslim invasions into Europe—but only for a time. New

York and Paris are now also the scenes of battle, but they will not be the last places we see similar things.

Thus, as a first step in understanding what we now face, consider the slaughter in Algeria. It awakened me to what the world is up against. In 1996 what happened to French monks at a monastery in the Atlas Mountains seemed but an isolated happening. Today it has become an everyday event someplace in the world.

When I recall in my mind this "incident", if it can be called by that neutral name, I am reminded of the comment that Robert Royal made in his book *The Catholic Martyrs of the Twentieth Century*.[3] Many of these people, Royal wrote, are killed in obscurity. No one notices them. They died bearing witness. I am mindful of the fifteenth chapter of John, which reads: "If the world hates you, know that it has hated me before it hated you. If you were of the world, the world would love its own; but because you are not of the world, but I chose you out of the world, therefore the world hates you. . . . If they persecuted me, they will persecute you" (18–20). This being hated simply for being what one is, it strikes me, is just about where we are, not only before the Muslim world, but before our own world with its Christian past now largely "hated". This book, then, is a record, a chronology of events and my efforts to understand them in the light of philosophy, in the light of Islam itself, and in the light of revelation—both Christian and Muslim.

---

[3] Robert Royal, *The Catholic Martyrs of the Twentieth Century* (New York: Crossroads, 2000).

The Seven Trappist Monks:
The World without Regret

One evening, during my retreat at an old Jesuit novitiate, I read an unforgettable letter in *L'Osservatore Romano*, English edition, June 12, 1996. In it, Dom Bernardo Olivera, the abbot general of the Cistercians of the Strict Observance, or Trappists, writes about the brutal, wholly arbitrary murder of seven Trappist monks in the Atlas Mountains of Algeria by the Muslim Groupe islamique armé (GIA) faction.

Dom Bernardo recalls that 1998 will mark the nine hundredth anniversary of the founding of Cîteaux. He mentions the many monks of his order killed in this century, especially those seven monks murdered in Algeria, plus the other Catholics, brothers, and nuns, slaughtered there and elsewhere for the same reason. He mentions John Paul II's reminder in *Tertio millennio adveniente* about the witness of martyrdom in the Church. "This is a witness not to be forgotten", Dom Bernardo stressed.

The immediate history of these seven monks, evidently very good and humble men, is recounted. They understood that they were in a dangerous area. The apostolic delegate, the archbishop, and one local Muslim official offered protection for them if they would move to more secure quarters.

Adapted from "Goodbye without Regret", *Crisis*, November 1, 1996, 58, http://www.crisismagazine.com/1996/sense-and-nonsense-goodbye-without-regret.

But the Trappists have a vow of stability. For several years they had considered their options, but each time decided to stay.

On December 29, 1993, one of the Trappists, Father Christopher, wrote a letter to the chief of the GIA cadre who had come threateningly to the monastery on Christmas Eve:

> Brother, allow me to address you like this, man to man, believer to believer. . . . In the present conflict . . . it seems to us impossible to take sides. The fact that we are foreigners forbids it. Our state as MONKS binds us to the choice of God for us, which is prayer and the simple life, manual work, hospitality and sharing with everyone, especially the poor. . . . These reasons for our life are a free choice for each one of us. They bind us until death. I do not think it is the will of God that this death should come to us through you.

Earlier this year, in March 1996, under a new GIA head, the monks were taken prisoner. They were accused of evangelizing. No First Amendment here. The emir stated, "Monks who live among the working classes can be legitimately killed." Once taken prisoner, the seven monks were in a new legal position: it was now licit to apply to them what applies to lifelong unbelievers when they are prisoners of war: murder, slavery, or exchange for Muslim prisoners.

The French had a prisoner that the emir wanted exchanged. He sent warnings to the French Foreign Office that, without the exchange, the monks would be executed. Next, the emir rationalized, "The choice is yours. If you liberate, we shall liberate; if you refuse, we will cut their throats. Praised be God."

In the end, the French president decided not to deal with such terrorists. The result was that on or around May 21,

1996, the monks were murdered in the gruesome manner indicated.

Dom Bernardo's letter, from which this account is taken, leaves little to the imagination. Yet something almost mystical is in this letter. We cannot help but think also of the unexpected passage on martyrdom in John Paul II's *Veritatis splendor*. Here we have faithful, peaceful men butchered for a legal subtlety, for the "praise of God", so the murderers claimed.

The account reads like classic tragedy, or more like the death of Saint Thomas More, whose murder, I believe, was shared by a few other monks and only one bishop.

The oldest of the murdered monks was Brother Luc, who was eighty during the monastic retreat of January 1994. Dom Bernardo had recalled a nun in Angola who, for her first vows, had chosen the reading for her Mass the passage about forgiveness of enemies. This meaning of receiving and forgiving seemed to explain these lives.

During the dinner ending the retreat, Brother Luc had played a cassette tape that he had been saving for his funeral. The song that he played was, incredibly, Edith Piaf's "Je ne regrette rien".

I find something more than a little poignant about an elderly Trappist brother murdered by a member of the GIA. By observing his law, the heartless believer slit the throat of a kindly old man, who, on his eightieth birthday, in his refectory, had listened to Edith Piaf sing the song that he wanted played for his funeral.

I have this tape of Edith Piaf singing "Je ne regrette rien". On listening to it now, I pray for these seven Trappist monks and the Muslims who slew them.

1

Hilaire Belloc on the "Apparently Unconvertible" Religion

I

One of the most difficult exercises in political prudence, I think, is philosophically to describe accurately a regime in the locale one is visiting, living, or encountering a formidable adversary. For, to delineate a regime correctly, we must have some criterion of judgment according to which we can decide whether any regime is good or bad. Without this standard—without a universal philosophy, in other words—we are engaged merely in name-calling without substance. This possibility of describing regimes *as they are* implies a universal political philosophy based on foundations independent of, though not unrelated to, actual regimes, and enough civic freedom to articulate such principles, meaning, without fear of prison or death for doing so.

As philosophers, beginning with Socrates, have led us to realize, this effort to examine the nature of a regime can be a dangerous exercise. Deviant princes and rulers, whatever we call them, do not like to know what they actually are. And citizens do not like to articulate the real nature of their

Adapted from "Belloc and the 'Apparently Unconvertible' Religion", *Vital Speeches of the Day* 69 (April 1, 2003), 375–82.

rulers, often themselves agreeing with the principles of their regime, a truth Plato taught us long ago when he spoke about the relation of our souls to our regimes. Princes and people prefer to be told that they themselves already embody the highest of moral norms, that they do God's will or are the "best regime", whatever it is they embody in fact according to classic philosophic standards. This endeavor to identify the type of polity before us becomes doubly difficult when the regime is also directly or indirectly said to be a regime that arises from or is devoted to the implementation of a rule rooted in a revelation or religion. In this case, we deal no longer with a regime as a mere political entity but with one that claims transcendent origins or justifications. The grounds for the truth of any revelation cannot be avoided.

Leo Strauss has noted that medieval Muslim philosophers, aware of this particular difficulty in pronouncing in public the theoretic character of a regime in which they lived, chose, for safety's sake, to do their philosophy in private. The philosopher externally did what was expected of him in terms of devotion and pious practices. But, even though he dissembled about religion in public, he preferred private philosophy to religion as an explanation of the truth of things. Indeed, that alternative to choose privacy in Islam was the philosophers' only viable alternative if they wanted to live and philosophize, albeit cautiously.

This move to philosophy meant, in Strauss' view, that the philosopher had to come up with a theory in which the presumed revelation that ruled the public order was itself subordinated to philosophy. Philosophy judged revelation. This judgment meant that the philosopher had to explain the purpose and the content of the revelation's terms on rational grounds alone. The explained terms of religious credibility —the political theology of the religion, in other words—

were unsustainable intellectually because they could not be fully understood by philosophy. The notion that the Qur'an, for example, is a book, the text of which was directly spoken to Muhammad in Arabic with no intermediary, is, even without examining the book's content for contradictory or false teachings, unbelievable on any rational grounds.

This task of letting the public life be Muslim, even if not credible, was accomplished by treating the way of life depicted in the Qur'an as a "myth" specifically and artfully designed to enable rulers to keep the intransigent masses in line. This understanding of myth was an ancient formula dating back at least to Epicurus. Aristotle himself said that the tyrant, if he wants to stay in power, should observe the local pious customs; he should keep the masses busy, exhausted, and entertained while not allowing anything to be spoken in private. A similar position occurred in late medieval Europe in what is known as Latin Averroism. This was the position that there were two "truths", one of revelation and one of reason. The two could contradict each other, whatever that view might eventually do to the unity of the human soul. We need not "reconcile" them. If everyone played the game, this theory allowed the philosopher to philosophize and the believer to believe with no worry about evident contradictions.

The myth of religion, thus, is useful politically, but it is not true or compatible with philosophy. The philosopher lived a secret or private life, as Socrates, in his *Apology*, affirmed that he also did, lest he be killed sooner. It is taken for granted that no vocal philosopher accused in the mythic religious polity will survive. These are the rules of the game. It was thus not possible that more than a few philosophers would know the falsity of the myth explaining the particular revelation and the difficulty in knowing the truth about our being conformed more or less to what we know about the opaqueness of human nature, with or without the notion of the Fall.[1] On the surface, all would be calm. Religion was in effect a useful way to control the inevitable turmoil in the masses, those who did not know or rule themselves. Philosophy and truth are not intended for everyone. It is instructive to recognize that when we come to Saint Thomas, it was first necessary for him to establish that revelation and philosophy were not contradictory to each other before the truths of revelation and reason could be coherently seen to belong to the same world of truth and reality. Unavoidably, this position also required some position on the very truth of the respective revelations.

II

Considering that, in many ways, Islam has been the oldest and most persistent enemy of Christianity, the one from which there is rarely a return if we look back at the lands once conquered by Muslim armies or traders in whatever century, it is surprising how little the official Church has said about Islam. Saint Thomas' *Summa contra gentiles* still seems like the major Christian effort to define what Islam is. Though Islam is a huge historical fact—the fastest-growing religion in the world today, including at least a fifth of the world population, with new mosques regularly appearing wherever they are permitted—we have, for example, no encyclical or letter entitled "What Is Islam?" We have nothing that parallels *Mit brennender Sorge* or *Divini Redemptoris*, no Syl-

---

[1] See Leo Strauss, *Persecution and the Art of Writing* (Westport, Conn.: Greenwood, 1973), 11–24; Ralph Lerner and Muhsin Mahdi, *Medieval Political Philosophy* (Ithaca: Cornell University Press, 1978), 1–21.

labus of Errors or canons of the Council of Trent. It is almost as if the Church has never considered the truth claims of Islam important. From a theological point of view, we trace multiple Christian heresies in our documents, but not Islam, which was, in a way, itself a Christian heresy. On the surface, this lack seems curious, almost as if Islam was not important enough to take seriously or there was a certain danger in doing so.

We do have, to be sure, recent exhortations about what we have in common with Islam and other religions. Our contemporary mode of approach is liberal and irenic—dialogue, when and if that is possible, never any confrontation, even when provoked. We are loath to mention any problem, including the vast numbers of Christians killed in Islamic countries in the past century, except when it is posed in the most general terms that often make the problems sound to be caused by Western ideology, not Muslim belief or practice. We impose Western philosophical or ideological methods of analysis on Islamic lands and expect this formula to explain their inner ethos. We use the scientific method, which blinds us to what is going on. In short, we dialogue not really with Muslims but with ourselves. It frightens us to hear ourselves called "infidels" by Muslims because of what we believe about God and Christ. It is not merely a case of exaggerated rhetoric but the definition of what seems to threaten Islam, namely, another understanding of God, particularly the Trinitarian God and the Incarnation. Much of the appeal of Islam seems to depend directly on the denial of this complex understanding of the Deity that we are bound to hold and propagate.

The twenty-first century, it seems clear, will more likely be a century of confrontation with world religions rather than with world ideologies, as was the twentieth century.

Few intellectuals expected this event. In terms of morals and vitality, the West has already declined. Roger Scruton's remark strikes home: "The intrusion of the media into the battlefield has had a shattering effect on the perception of war. And the declining birthrate and increasing longevity of the population have made Western societies ever more reluctant to risk in combat their dwindling supply of sons."[2] An abundant supply of sons is something that Islam has, many of whom seem surprisingly willing to die defending or expanding it. Muslim, Hindu, Chinese, and Buddhist movements seem to have grown stronger, not weaker, during the supposedly skeptical twentieth century.

Christian populations are under pressure in India, in China, in Buddhist and Muslim lands. Many Christians in these lands leave voluntarily, although usually under pressure to do so. Most of the Christians once in Arab lands are now in the West. They voted with their feet. Meanwhile, the Muslim presence, due in part to their comparative increase in numbers, is found everywhere in Europe and America, along with Chinese, Hindu, Buddhist, and other representatives of various world religions. The modern secularist seems almost like a cultural oddity confined to small academic enclaves in small corners of the world. It is ironic that much of modern political philosophy was premised on the notion of reducing the importance of religion to prevent religious and civil wars. In the light of the stringent closure of these religions in on themselves in their historical locations, together with their lack of any real sense of religious freedom based on the dignity of the person, the alternative of skepticism or atheism almost seems healthy in comparison with the lands in which there is no escape, ex-

[2] Roger Scruton, *The West and the Rest: Globalization and the Terrorist Threat* (Wilmington: ISI Books, 2002), 59.

cept perhaps inward, as in the case of the medieval Muslim philosophers.

III

In this light, it may be of some merit to take a further look at Hilaire Belloc's discussions of the future of Islam made back in the 1930s. What is remarkable about Belloc's comments on Islam, as we read them today, is his ability to judge historical trends on the basis of a spiritual force or power. Though he was a soldier and a military historian who loved the knowledge of battles and battlefields, generals and soldiers, Belloc never thought that it was material power that ultimately determined what would happen among men and civilizations. "Cultures spring from religions; ultimately the vital force which maintains any culture is its philosophy, its attitude towards the universe; the decay of a religion involves the decay of the culture corresponding to it—we see that most clearly in the breakdown of Christendom today."[3] He is aware that, for some three hundred years after the Battle of Vienna on September 11, 1683, the Muslim lands had gradually dropped out of the modern picture as serious threats. They were seen to be backward lands, and in fact were backward. In spite of the oil, whose value they had little or nothing to do with, this is still largely the case.

Yet, Belloc was aware that Islam did not change in spite of centuries of Western influence. When it came to the fundamentals, Islam was utterly unaffected by Western occupation. As Belloc wrote in *Survivals and New Arrivals*:

---

[3] Hilaire Belloc, *The Great Heresies* (San Francisco: Ignatius Press, 2017), 99.

We thought of its [Islam's] religion as a sort of fossilized thing about which we need not trouble. That was almost certainly a mistake. We shall almost certainly have to reckon with Islam in the near future. Perhaps if we lose our Faith it will rise. For after this subjugation of the Islamic culture by nominally Christian nations had already been achieved, the political conquerors of that culture began to notice two disquieting features about it. The first was that its spiritual foundation proved immovable; the second that its area of occupation did not recede, but on the contrary slowly expanded.[4]

Suffice it to say, we are reckoning with Islam today. Europe and much of America did largely lose the faith, as Belloc observed even before World War II, and Islam is expanding there. The expansion of Islam is also occurring in Africa and Asia.

The solidity of Islam, its inner coherence, whatever its cause and the methods by which it was kept, struck Belloc. As he wrote in the same book,

Islam would not look at any Christian missionary effort. The so-called Christian Governments, in contact with it, it spiritually despised. The ardent and sincere Christian missionaries were received usually with courtesy, sometimes with fierce attack, but were never allowed to affect Islam. I think it true to say that Islam is the only spiritual force on earth which Catholicism has found an impregnable fortress. Its votaries are the one religious body conversions from which are insignificant.[5]

Belloc made a similar observation in *The Great Heresies*:

[4] Hilaire Belloc, *Survivals and New Arrivals* (New York: MacMillan, 1929), 252.
[5] Ibid.

Islam is apparently *unconvertible*. The missionary efforts made by great Catholic orders which have been occupied in trying to turn Mohammedans into Christians for nearly four hundred years have everywhere wholly failed. We have in some places driven the Mohammedan master out and freed his Christian subjects from Mohammedan control, but we have had hardly any effect in converting individual Mohammedans.[6]

Belloc recognized that Islam flourished because it did have some basic truth about God, however that be interpreted. "Mohammedanism struck permanent roots, developing a life of its own, and became at last something like a new religion", he wrote in *The Great Heresies*. "Like all heresies, Mohammedanism lived by the Catholic truths which it had retained. Its insistence on personal immortality, on the Unity and Infinite Majesty of God, on His Justice and Mercy, its insistence on the equality of human souls in the sight of their Creator—these were its strength."[7] Belloc saw the strength of Islam in its virtues.

It is for this reason alone, the impregnability of Islam to Catholicism, however, that the Church needs to take more cognizance of this growing force in the world. It is not enough to condemn violence in the abstract. "Go forth and teach all nations" is not possible if the nations will not allow themselves to be preached to. The Western theories of freedom of religion, whether secular or religious, have made no headway in Islam, and only rarely is it criticized for this lack. Those few who are Christians or members of other religions, in most Muslim lands, in practice must be content to remain second-class citizens and are constantly subject to the pressure to convert to Islam.

[6] Belloc, *The Great Heresies*, 73.
[7] Ibid., 96.

IV

Belloc's thesis is that Islam began as a Christian heresy that retained the Jewish side of the faith, the oneness and omnipotence of God, but denied all the Christian aspects—the Incarnation, the divinity of Christ, who, as a result, became just a prophet. The denial of the Church, the priesthood, and the sacraments followed. Islam succeeded because, in its own terms, it was a simple religion. It was easy to understand and follow its few doctrinal and devotional points. The expansion of Islam was almost always by arms; after each conquest, the Muslim caliphs or sultans ruled. They were intolerant, but they more or less accepted political submission in return for tribute. At least twice in the history of the West, Islam almost overran Europe, once at Poitiers in the eighth century and once at Vienna in the seventeenth century.

Interestingly, the Church since that period has celebrated certain feast days precisely in memory of these victories, the most notable of which is Saint Pius V's establishment of the Feast of the Holy Rosary on October 7, 1571. This feast commemorated the naval victory at Lepanto. "The name of Lepanto should remain in the minds of all men with a sense of history as one of the half dozen great names in the history of the Christian world."[8] In these days of apologizing for practically everything, one wonders if some pope someday will not rescind this feast on grounds of goodwill. The cynic might hope that we at least wait until Islam first apologizes for the initial slaughter and conquest of Christian lands from Spain to Africa and Asia.

These earlier popes, in any case, understood that they had

[8] Ibid., 92.

an enemy and that they were blessed not to have fallen under Muslim army rulers. Urban II's call for the Crusades, though much misunderstood, can largely be judged as a belated and mainly unsuccessful effort of the European Christians to defend themselves against Islam. Belloc, in fact, thought that the Crusaders were from the beginning undermanned and rather poorly led, though often with much heroism. Their final defeat at the hands of Saladin at Hattin in 1187 he considered to be one of the most significant battles in the history of the world because it confirmed Muslim rule across a wide stretch of the world, most of which it still controls.

Unlike Stanley Jaki, Belloc did not think that there was something in Islamic theology that militated against Islam's ever becoming a major industrial or military-technological power by itself. The fact that it never accomplished this transformation was for Belloc merely an accident, whereas for Jaki it was rooted in the relation of an absolute notion of divine will to its consequent denial of stable secondary causes. Jaki saw much of the rage in modern Islam to be due to its failure or inability to modernize itself by its own powers.[9] Most of the weapons and equipment found in Muslim states are still foreign made, usually inferior, and paid for with oil money.

The "new" weapon that Islam displayed on September 11, 2001, was a kind of fanatic willingness to use any method of terror even if it costs the lives of individuals who are often popularly considered to be "martyrs" for killing infidels. This method needs little technology. The West has minimum moral equipment with which to respond to such tactics. Indeed, as both Aristotle and Machiavelli saw, if someone does not fear for his own life, it is very difficult to stop

---

[9] Stanley L. Jaki, *The Road of Science and the Ways to God* (Chicago: University of Chicago Press, 1978), 35–36.

him. But neither of them thought of the idea of sacrificing one's life specifically for this purpose. Indeed, in the history of the West, Islam has always sent a kind of terror through the hearts of those on its borders who were about to be attacked or through the hearts of those who had to live under its control. Belloc alludes to this phenomenon:

> These things being so, the recrudescence of Islam, the possibility of that terror under which we lived for centuries reappearing, and of our civilization again fighting for its life against what was its chief enemy for a thousand years, seems fantastic. Who in the Mohammedan world today can manufacture and maintain the complicated instruments of modern war? Where is the political machinery whereby the religion of Islam can play an equal part in the modern world?[10]

The question seems less rhetorical today because numbers, in the end, count, as does the willingness of people to die using modern machinery like normal airplanes to carry out what is attested to be a religious mission, however much we choose to identify it as simply "terrorism" without a cause. What is also true is that this terrorism, or its threat, is now everywhere. Thus far, at least, we see within Islam itself little effort to control its own "terrorists" or to sympathize with those who suffer from them or who must defend themselves against them.

The inconvertibility of Islam leads us to several perhaps radical reflections. It is a common saying among Christians that the blood of martyrs is the seed of the faith. There have been many, many Christian martyred by Islam over the centuries and currently. As in the case of the slaughter of the

[10] Belloc, *The Great Heresies*, 98.

Armenians by the Turks, there will always appear some justification—the Christian blasphemed Allah. The very existence of Christianity is a blasphemy in Muslim terms if
we insist on the truth of the Incarnation, that God became
man. These historical martyrdoms appear to have had little
or no effect in terms either of conversion or even acknowl-
edgment by us.

Moreover, we have the parallel phenomenon of the Muslim martyr, the man who kills in the name of Allah, whether
by detonating a suicide vest in a church in the Philippines,
by slitting the throats of French Trappist monks in Algeria
on Christmas Eve, or by flying planes into the World Trade
Center. In some basic sense, these killers are pictured as martyrs. Nor is the notion of "holy war" unknown in Islam.
However much the Church tries to argue that such actions
cannot be considered to be justified, still within at least some
significant branches of Muslim opinion, those who commit
these actions are considered to be genuine martyrs seeking
to defend or propagate the religion and therefore worthy of
Allah. When we try to oppose this position on, say, natural
law terms, we find that our mode of discourse is itself alien
to what much of Islam conceives itself to be. The basis of
our arguments is not admitted to be valid.

Belloc thought that Islam began as a heresy and became a
new religion culturally when it had to account for and explain its successes on the field of battle. The stunning successes on the field of battle had to be administered.

> Mohammedanism was a *heresy*: that is the essential point to
> grasp before going any further. It began as a heresy, not as a
> new religion. It was not a pagan contrast with the Church:
> it was not an alien enemy. It was a perversion of Chris-
> tian doctrine. Its vitality and endurance soon gave it the

appearance of a new religion, but those who were contemporary with its rise saw it for what it was—not a denial, but an adaptation and misuse, of the Christian thing.[11]

As most scholars recognize, the main parts of what Islam took from revelation are from Judaism rather than Christianity. Islam kept much of what Christianity has in common with Judaism—the transcendence of Yahweh, creation, divine justice and punishment, the devotion of the people to God.

But Islam was itself not like Arianism and other early heresies. It arose from without the ancient Christian world. For it, Christ was not God but rather a human prophet. This is the explicit denial of the root principle of Christianity.

> With that denial of the Incarnation went the whole sacramental structure. He [the Muslim] refused to know anything of the Eucharist, with its Real Presence; he stopped the sacrifice of the Mass, and therefore the institution of a special priesthood. In other words, he, like so many other lesser heresiarchs, founded his heresy on simplification.[12]

Though it is not often attended to, saying Mass itself is forbidden in Saudi Arabia, even in private. When the Mass is permitted in other Muslim lands, it is restricted and constantly hemmed in by various formal and informal practices. Freedom of religion is not a concept that rises naturally in Muslim theory but is a Western idea, even largely a modern Western idea. In Islam, the very practice of freedom of religion is thought to be a species of not giving submission to Allah, even where some non-Muslim worship is permitted.

[11] Ibid., 59–60.
[12] Ibid., 61–62.

Belloc thought that Islam expanded rapidly for the very good reason that it won battles. This success should give modern pacifists pause, but it usually does not. Yet, to call Islam a religion of simplicity is, in Belloc's terms, rather a compliment. He notes that it freed many people from the complicated clutch of usury, from the lawyers. It freed slaves if they converted and made them brothers within the system. The brotherhood of faith trumps other relationships. Belloc distinguished between the character of the spread of Islam initially in the Near East and that expansion into Persian and Mongol lands—the area from Mesopotamia to India and the Eastern Roman Empire. "The uniformity of temper which is the mark of Asiatic society responded at once to this new idea of one very simple, personal form of government, sanctified by religion, and ruling with a power theoretically absolute from one centre."[13] It was from these conquests that Islam learned of Greek philosophy and other cultures, the origin of much of its science and art. "Islam was the one heresy", Belloc wrote, "that nearly destroyed Christendom through its early material and intellectual superiority."[14]

Much has been made of the "tolerance" in Islam, especially for religions of the Book. This tolerance was often merely the inability to change large conquered populations in a short time. Belloc thought that "the Mohammedan temper was not tolerant. It was, on the contrary, fanatical and bloodthirsty. It felt no respect for, nor even curiosity about, those from whom it differed. It was absurdly vain of itself, regarding with contempt the high Christian culture about

[13] Ibid., 66.
[14] Ibid., 68.

it. It still so regards it even today."[15] The practical compromise in this situation was to allow the Christians to remain but within very confined areas and occupations. They had to pay a tribute. Many were gradually absorbed into Islam since they saw no hope of escaping it.

V

This record of Islam's own consistency, its closed nature, its remaining itself had to be reconsidered in some detail, Belloc thought. It has been "the most formidable of the heresies." The question is now, why has it survived? "Millions of modern people of the white civilization—that is, the civilization of Europe and America—have forgotten all about Islam."[16] This could be written in 1938, but not in 2003. The question that must now be asked is not merely "Why has it survived?" but "Why has it flourished?" Belloc can only be said to have foreseen the problem: "It is, in fact, the most formidable and persistent enemy which our civilization has had, and may at any moment become as large a menace in the future as it has been in the past."[17] Neither our modern culture nor the modern Church allows us this frankness.

Usually, Belloc thought, heresies make an initial impact and then decline and disappear. Islam did not do this. When Islam was defeated, it remained strong in numbers and in convictions. How then is Islam different? Some Westerners say it is because it is simple and founded on justice and improves on Christianity. Belloc did not accept this reason

[15] Ibid., 69.
[16] Ibid., 71.
[17] Ibid.

because other heresies maintain the same thing, but they still fade; not Islam. Historically, Islam constantly gained new recruits: the Turk, the Mongol.

> The causes of this vitality [of Islam] are very difficult to explore, and perhaps cannot be reached. For myself I should ascribe it in some part to the fact that Mohammedanism being a thing from the outside, a heresy that did not arise from within the body of the Christian community but beyond its frontiers, has always possessed a reservoir of men, newcomers pouring in to revivify its energies. But this cannot be a full explanation.[18]

Today, I suspect, they gain new recruits largely from their own population growth, which expands to fill the vacuum left by the low birthrates in the West. The Crusades did not split Islam geographically. Belloc held that if the Crusades (1095–1200) had cut Africa off from Asia, Islam may have declined. It is interesting how many of the advocates of occupation of Iraq today use this theory of the need to split Islam and hence reduce its geopolitical power.

Yet, Belloc maintained that, though based on the army, Islam did have a cultural force.

> The success of Mohammedanism had not been due to its offering something more satisfactory in the way of philosophy and morals, but, as I have said, to the opportunity it afforded of freedom to the slave and debtor, and an extreme simplicity which pleased the unintelligent masses who were perplexed by the mysteries inseparable from the profound intellectual life of Catholicism, and from its radical doctrine of the Incarnation.[19]

---

[18] Ibid., 97.
[19] Ibid., 78.

This position is not unlike that of Eric Voegelin, who argued that the susceptibility of Western Christians to modern ideology was due to the practical disbelief of many Christians in the ultimate transcendent goal of the faith.[20]

Belloc, in fact, saw a relation between the failure of the Crusades and the rise of modern Europe, which at first turned in on itself before finding the technological means of bypassing Islamic lands with the discoveries of America and the sea route to Asia. Belloc even held that the success of the Reformation in part was due to the defeat of Catholic and papal policies in the Crusades. (Belloc's book *The Crusades* remains one of the most poignant accounts of the failed enterprise.)

> Had the Crusaders' remaining force at the end of the first Crusading march been a little more numerous, had they taken Damascus and the string of towns on the fringe of the desert, the whole history of the world would have been changed. The world of Islam would have been cut in two, with the East unable to approach the West.[21]

North Africa, the old Roman lands, was not recovered. "They failed, but they made modern Europe", wrote Belloc. The Reformation was due to the weakness at the center, the loss of unity as modern nations formed.

What Belloc was most conscious of, however, was that, unlike Islam, Christianity did not retain its inner coherence, its faith. "Christian Europe is and should be by nature one; but it has forgotten its nature in forgetting its religion."[22] Belloc connected this loss of inner coherence in the West to

---

[20] Eric Voegelin, *Science, Politics, and Gnosticism* (Chicago: Regnery/Gateway, 1968), 109.

[21] Belloc, *The Great Heresies*, 86.

[22] Ibid., 95–96.

the opportunity for Islam to rise again. It is partly due to the downplaying of the importance of religion in the West that it has been unable or unwilling to understand the attraction of Islam in its own inner coherence. "It has always seemed to me possible, and even probable," Belloc wrote,

> that there would be a resurrection of Islam and that our sons or our grandsons would see the renewal of that tremendous struggle between the Christian culture and what has been for more than a thousand years its greatest opponent. . . .
> . . . The future always comes as a surprise, but political wisdom consists in attempting at least some partial judgment of what that surprise may be. And for my part I cannot but believe that a main unexpected thing of the future is the return of Islam. Since religion is at the root of all political movements and changes and since we have here a very great religion physically paralyzed but morally intensely alive, we are in the presence of an unstable equilibrium which cannot remain permanently unstable.[23]

It is interesting that even with the return of Islam to the forefront of our consciousness, we do not want to see this return as a religious thing explained in terms of Islam itself.

VI

How are we to assess these potent reflections of Belloc? Stretched halfway across the world, Islam is divided up into many "nations", though that concept of nationalism is not an Islamic idea. The central organs of the Church seem to be against doing anything radical about any Islamic threat, preferring diplomacy and not forcefully noting the widespread

[23] Ibid., 95–96.

attacks on Christians throughout the world. It is interesting that several Vatican officials give as a reason for not using force the fear of the rising up of Islam and the potential terror it can cause everywhere in the world. They are right; the danger is real. Normally, this view would be an argument for doing something about the problem when we can, before something more terrible happens, particularly if the problem lies in Islam itself and its inability to accept the normal peaceful structures of society. Almost all the minor wars today have some Islamic component. Within Islam, there are various schools of interpretation from the well-financed Wahhabi extremists in Saudi Arabia to the more mild versions of some Shiites.

Geopoliticians and theologians alike argue that, since we really have no common philosophy, we must seek ways to reinterpret Islam within itself, using its own texts and traditions to mollify the extremists, who now see an opportunity to establish Muslim dominance all over the world. At first sight, this seems preposterous. But as Belloc said, surprising things happen, like the rise of Islam, or Christianity, or Judaism in the first place. It makes us wonder whether there is not something objective to be said for the reality of salvation history after all.

For Catholics in particular, Belloc's estimate was sobering. He lived before "ecumenism", but he certainly wondered about its effectiveness in the case of Islam, however politically wise it might be to proceed as the Muslim philosophers and not mention any truths outside the Qur'an. "Missionary effort has had no appreciable effect on it [Islam]", Belloc concluded.

> It still converts pagan savages wholesale. It even attracts from time to time some European eccentric, who joins its

body. *But the Mohammedan never becomes a Catholic.* No fragment of Islam ever abandons its sacred book, its code of morals, its organized system of prayer, its simple doctrine.

In view of this, anyone with a knowledge of history is bound to ask himself whether we shall not see in the future a rival of Mohammedan political power, and the renewal of the old pressure of Islam on Christendom.[24]

These words are strong and historically true. They also today strike us as prophetic. Few paid much attention to Belloc in his time. Although in our own day Muslims do sometimes convert to Christianity, the fact remains that conversion is forbidden in countries ruled by Islamic law and difficult to effect for social and cultural reasons outside the Muslim world.[25]

In the end, I cannot help but have a gratefulness to the "apparently unconvertible religion", to radical Islam, for waking us up. We could make the case that all our studies, all our concern with Western ideology and power may have been misplaced. What we should have been paying attention to is our souls and what is the best explanation of our existence and destiny. Islam has another soul and another destiny that it seeks to spread, by its own proven means, to the ends of the earth, an idea that it probably got, ironically, from the end of the Gospel of Matthew.

---

[24] Ibid., 97. Emphasis in the original.
[25] Conversions from Christianity to Islam and from Islam to Christianity occur in Asia, Africa, the Near East, and among immigrants to Europe and North America. Websites listing these movements can easily be found on the Internet.

2

On Islam

Zenit reported that at the Great Mosque in Rome a Muslim cleric called for the annihilation of "the enemies of Islam and [a] guarantee everywhere in the world [of] the victory of the Nation of Islam".[1] This outburst caused the raising of not a few Italian eyebrows. In America, former Fox News commentator Bill O'Reilly, among others, holds that World War III has already begun. War with whom? With Islam. But what Islam will fight a world war?

Islam is a religion. No major military force exists in Islamic lands. Islam is composed of perhaps a billion believers. Almost no record, except isolated cases, exists of conversions from Islam to any other religion or to secular philosophy. Christianity has never made a dent. Conversions go the other way. Muslim believers are concentrated into some twenty-two nations. Members of the religion have almost complete control. A large presence, not the majority, of Muslim believers is found in India and China. Increasingly,

---

Adapted from "On Islam", *Crisis*, January 1, 2004, 63, http://www.crisismag azine.com/2004/sense-and-nonsense-on-islam.

[1] "In Rome, a Muslim's Call for a 'Holy War' Raises Concern", Zenit, June 13, 2003, https://zenit.org/articles/in-rome-a-muslim-s-call-for-a-holy -war-raises-concern/.

Muslims inhabit almost every Western country, especially those with declining and aging populations.

The form of polity in Muslim nations betrays common signs of arbitrary military rule: civil intolerance of other religions and practices, and usually poverty. Few, if any, Muslim nations could be called free societies. In these areas the term "tolerance" means something different from our accustomed understanding. A non-Muslim can survive but only as a second-class citizen, however delicately it is put. Anyone familiar with modern martyrs notes that there are a disproportionate number of them in Muslim lands. What complicates this figure is that the Muslim "terrorists", who are killed or kill themselves in bombings or fights, usually, along with local public opinion, consider themselves to be martyrs in the name of Islam.

The common Western doctrine, formulated by President George W. Bush as a rationale in the war against "terrorism", is that Islam is a peaceful religion. But somehow, with no connection to the religion, a large group of "terrorists", maybe 10 percent of the total, actively support this violent group. Most of the current wars or insurrections in the world today have a Muslim component. Strategists have been hard-pressed to define, in classical terms, this new kind of national and international threat. It does not appear to come directly from what is called a nation-state, even an Islamic one. Some Islamic states, however, support, finance, or protect such nationless "terrorists".

In an audience with the Catholic hierarchy of Egypt, Pope John Paul II remarked:

> The dialogue with Islam is particularly important in your country where this is the religion of the majority, but it also sets an example for the dialogue between the great world religions, which is vital following the tragic events linked

to terrorism that marked the beginning of the third millennium and whose causes public opinion might be tempted to ascribe to religion. I would like to remind you how essential it is that the world religions join forces to denounce terrorism and to work together at the service of justice, peace and brotherhood among men and women.[2]

Evidently, the pope thinks only "erroneous" public opinion holds that this problem has anything to do with Islam as a religion. While not denying self-defense, he does not, unfortunately, indicate whether he thinks that "denouncing terrorism" by world religions will in fact prevent attacks.

The *Economist* of London published a long survey, "In the Name of Islam", covering the whole Muslim world, to try to come up with a balanced view of the nature of the threat. The survey acknowledged a real problem that cannot be misjudged:

> When people are trying to kill you, especially when they are good at it, it is prudent to listen to the reasons they give. And Mr. Bin Laden launched his "war" explicitly in Islam's name. Indeed, three years before the Twin Towers, he went to the trouble of issuing a lengthy "Declaration of World Islamic Front for Jihad against the Jews and the Crusaders," stating that "to kill Americans and their allies, both civil and military, is the individual duty of every Muslim who is able."[3]

This is heady stuff. The *Economist* did not find a world plot exactly and tried to trace various motives for trouble not rooted in such terrorist rhetoric.

What do I conclude from this? No more serious problem exists than the accurate answer to the question "What

[2] John Paul II, Address to the Catholic Hierarchy of Egypt (August 30, 2003), 7.
[3] "In the Name of Islam", *Economist*, September 13, 2003.

is Islam?'' Not a few Muslims have already decided the answer to this question. We call them "terrorists". Our own ideologies often prevent us from seeing anything except our own theories. The Holy Father and others insist that another way to resolve this issue, besides war and military defense, exists. This too is a theory. To work, we require an Islamic theory that can accept the premises of the papal theory. This is what is lacking. We could use an incisive encyclical, *On Islam*.

3

On Martyrdom and Suicide Bombers

After the London subway bombings (July 7, 2005), the father of Mohamed Atta, the lead suicide pilot in the World
Trade Center destruction, denounced as traitors those fellow Muslims who condemned these "terrorist" bombings.
He would encourage more attacks. Indeed, he would donate
$5,000 (such is the apparent cost of such acts) to carry out
another such bombing. That is how much, he thought, it
would take to finance another London attack, another "vol-
unteer" to kill others by killing himself.

Suicide Bombers Treated as Martyrs

A July 30, 2005, report in the London *Spectator* depicted the
in absentia funeral in Pakistan of one of the London suicide
bombers, Shehzad Tanweer. The Qur'an was read; a large
crowd was present. Tanweer was popularly considered a
"martyr" for his "heroic" act that killed seven people. It is

Adapted from "Martyrs and Suicide Bombers", *Ignatius Insight*, August 24,
2005, http://www.ignatiusinsight.com/features2005/schall_martyrsbombers
_aug05.asp.

this topic that I wish to discuss—the notion that a suicide bomber is a "martyr", a hero, to be imitated and encouraged, while those who oppose such actions, even if they are Muslim, are condemned.

In his August 20, 2005, address to Muslim leaders in Cologne, Benedict XVI, seeking some common ground between Muslims and Christians, remarked,

> I am certain that I echo your own thoughts when I bring up one of our concerns as we notice the spread of terrorism. . . . Terrorist activity is continually recurring in various parts of the world, plunging people into grief and despair . . .
>
> [T]errorism of any kind is a perverse and cruel choice which shows contempt for the sacred right to life and undermines the very foundations of all civil coexistence.[1]

Presumably, suicide bombings are a subset of "terrorism", itself an abstract word that avoids the explanation of "by whom?" and "for what purpose?"

The question is, does this "common ground" exist, and if so, what is its basis? Clearly, no common ground exists between the positive promotion of and the absolute condemnation of suicide bombing. Either it is right or wrong. If it is wrong, any organization or movement promoting it as a matter of principle and policy cannot be a valid religion or philosophy, no matter how earnest or sincere its proponents may be. Are those Muslims who do have "common ground" with Christians and Jews in condemning suicide bombings—say, on the basis of "rights" or natural law or reason—also thought to be "heretics" by accepted Muslim standards? Ought suicide bombing to be encouraged under any conceivable circumstances?

[1] Benedict XVI, Address to Representatives of Some Muslim Communities (Cologne, Germany, August 20, 2005).

This claim of the moral approval of suicide bombing, clearly found within uncomfortably large segments of Islam, is surely the point of many Muslims calling a suicide bomber a martyr. Historically, a martyr was not and could not be a suicide. Even Socrates at his trial had to explain why his acceptance of death at the hands of the state, even his self-administration of the death penalty, was not a suicide. Nor was Christ's voluntary crucifixion a suicide. In fact, a martyr is the exact opposite of a suicide bomber. A martyr is someone who upholds—by his *being unjustly killed*—the Socratic principle that it is never right to do wrong, even to oneself, no less to others.

More bluntly, a suicide bomber, by any objective standard, *cannot* be a martyr, though he may be the cause of the martyrdom of others. Both John Paul II and Benedict XVI have said that such deeds can never be justified by reason or religion, even when some religions or sects evidently do so justify them. A line is drawn in the sand. To approve and foster suicide bombing is to make something intrinsically evil to appear as good. This position has serious implications. Positive advocacy of suicide bombing, not to mention terrorist bombing that does not include suicide, indicates that the teaching of persons or groups holding the doctrine supporting it cannot be true.

Muslim Ambivalence?

Italian journalist Sandro Magister, in a long essay, charted the connection between the leaders of Muslim groups in Germany—with headquarters in Cologne and Munich— and the Muslim Brotherhood with its Egyptian and Syrian networks. Indeed, we know that at least some of the World Trade Center attacks were originally planned in Germany.

> In 1994, a frequent visitor of the mosque in Munich, Mahmoud Abouhalima, was given a life sentence in the United States for having organized, one year before, the car bomb attack on the World Trade Center in New York. But it was only after the collapse of the Twin Towers on September 11, 2001, that investigations into the connections between terrorism and the radical Islamic circle in Germany intensified.[2]

In a 2005 BBC *Panorama* debate about whether the British Muslim community refuses to look at the extremists among them, the leading British Muslim politician, Sir Iqbal Sacranie, "condemned suicide bombings by British Muslims anywhere and said there was no difference between the life of a Palestinian and the life of a Jew and that all life was sacred." But just to confuse things, in a separate interview, a senior spokesman for one of the Muslim Council of Britain's main affiliates, the Muslim Association of Britain, appeared to "condone the glorification of suicide bombers".[3] Numerous Muslim sources can be cited as approving this latter view.

Led by Prime Minister Tony Blair and President George Bush, Western leaders, both religious and political, have sought valiantly to maintain the separation between "peaceful" Muslims and terrorism. This distinction implies that only "peaceful" Muslims are "really" Muslims, if this liberal

---

[2] Sandro Magister, "From Cologne to the Conquest of Europe: How the Muslim Brotherhood Is Challenging the Pope", *Chiesa*, August 18, 2005, http://chiesa.espresso.repubblica.it/articolo/37837?eng=y.

[3] "Muslim Leaders 'in Denial' Claim", BBC, August 21, 2005, http://news.bbc.co.uk/2/hi/uk_news/4166402.stm.

and theological distinction is correct. Unfortunately, the terrorists themselves do claim with considerable historical and doctrinal evidence, on Qur'anic grounds, that they are in fact the true interpreters of Islam. In one sense, it is "illiberal" not to take them at their word. One of the problems with understanding Islam is that it has no final authority within itself to decide which of these two interpretations is valid. For every fatwa that pronounces suicide bombing wrong, another from an equally credible source pronounces it valid. This situation is perhaps why Blair and others are more and more insisting that Muslims, so that they can be held accountable, stand up and be counted in public as rejecting terrorism not only as a practice but as inherent in Islamic sources.

The test of Pius XII was Nazism. The test of John Paul II was Communism and absolutist liberalism. The test of Benedict XVI, for better or for worse, is Islam—and this in the context of whether or not the absolutist liberal theory can tame it. But Islam, unlike Nazism and Communism, and likewise unlike many academic analyses of it, is not primarily understood in terms of Western (often German) philosophical or social movements. Indeed, attempts to understand what is going on by these categories is more likely to obscure the truth than to clarify it.

By its record and its own theological presuppositions, Islam itself does not have and does not seek to have a regime of neutrality or tolerance. Its civil polities now and historically unite Islam and the state in various configurations. What Islam requires of non-Muslims within areas it politically controls, as Bat Ye'or has graphically shown in *Eurabia*, is subservience. Jews and Christians may be given a special place of subservience, sometimes called tolerance, but it is still subservience. The Copts in Egypt are perhaps the longest-lasting example of this.[4] The persecution of Christians in Sudan is the most graphic example.

The Final Goal

The first step in dealing with any movement or religion is to know what it is, what it holds about itself. Often, to be sure, a difference can be found between what one says one holds and what one holds to act on or practice. But not a few thinkers, like Hitler or Lenin, did tell us what they held and what they intended to do before they went ahead and did it. No one believed them until after they did what they told us that they intended to do.

In this sense, Muhammad and Islam itself, in word and action, do tell us what they have done and what they intend to do, if they could. One can say with little doubt that Europe today was intended by Islamic warriors to be Muslim. Europe, as Africa and the Middle East, was invaded for that purpose. And this purpose was conceived to be a religious purpose; the armies were fulfilling a mission. This goal is still held to be the purpose of the Muslim factions called "terrorists". The only reason Europe is not Muslim today is that Muslim armies were defeated by hard-fought military action in France and Austria. Many Islamic thinkers insist that any area that was taken back from Muslim control (Spain, for instance) is still theirs. There is no legitimate "taking back", something that makes the 2004 Spanish elections three days after Spain's own terrorist bombings doubly ironic.

---

[4] See *First Things*, March 2005, 47–50.

Moreover, most of the world that is officially Muslim to-day is Muslim because of long strings of military victories and conquests that have remained to form, in one way or an-other, present Islamic configurations. This situation is simply a fact, whatever we make of it. Terrorist actions today are generally formulated in terms either of winning back for-mer Muslim lands (Spain, Israel, the Balkans) or of pursu-ing the Muslim goal of peace, by which is meant the whole world under Muslim law. This rule indeed would be a kind of "peace" with all external opposition eliminated.

The present Islamic division between the "world of war" (non-Muslim lands) and the "world of peace" would be eliminated. No doubt, the unexpected rise of a visibly mil-itant Islam in recent decades is the result of certain Muslim theoreticians who see the West as morally weak and degen-erate, unwilling or unable to resist a concentrated attack, in-spired by suicide bombers. The fact that no reputable Mus-lim army is capable of fighting well-equipped troops, as the two Iraq wars show, does not mean no war exists. Rather, it means that we have an unlimited or unrestricted war that is fought with unconventional weapons.

The only thing really new today is that Islam, if patient, might well take over Europe and other areas through a com-bination of self-inflicted, rapid population decline among European peoples and continued rapid increase of Muslim birthrates in this area. This drama should be of especial in-terest to Catholics who once doubted the relevance of *Hu-manae vitae*. In this light, it now appears as one of the most im-portant documents of the twentieth century. In this sense, it is conceivable that Islam may not succeed precisely be-cause it did not follow the "peaceful" population route but provoked the one power capable of using systematic force against it. But it remains to be seen whether a long-term po-litical will to oppose the terrorist agenda can be sustained in democracies. The terrorists themselves seem sufficiently sophisticated to realize that the war is one not just of armies but of ideas and nightly news.

Little can be done about any dangerous threat until clarity about its nature is forthcoming. And even when its reality is recognized—I think of the Munich agreements or the control of Eastern Europe by the Soviets after World War II—the will and decision to do something about it must follow intelligence, assuming it is accurate. A German publisher has famously described contemporary Europe as a continent that completely lacks courage to face what threatens it. The vaunted European "diplomacy" to use "other" means than force, as in the case of trying to convince Iran not to produce nuclear weapons, is simply not effective.

The Horror of Terrorist "Martyrdom"

Perhaps nothing has needed clarification more at every level, from theological to political to medical to commonsensical, than the difference between suicide bombing and martyrdom. It seems almost obscene to see them linked together as manifestations of the same thing. We should begin by affirming that the Muslim apologists and those who follow them do hold that suicide bombing is martyrdom. It is an act chosen to further their destiny with Allah by killing themselves and others in a "cause" of furthering Muslim goals that are at the same time political and theological. Whatever we think of this view, it is held either actively or in sympathy by a large part of the Muslim world. Few within the Muslim world itself—though there are those who do—voice much effective criticism of this association of suicide and martyrdom.

It is well and good for us cynically to think, using our own uncomprehending categories, that for the various bin Ladens of this world this suicide bombing is just a form of realpolitik, with no religious overtone. We might reinforce our view by noting that few al-Qaida leaders themselves have been suicide bombers, though not a few have been shot by various military and police forces, both Muslim and American. Suicide bombing is definitely an instrument of war, but that does not, in theological terms, prevent it also from being something like an act of devotion, a martyrdom. Wars can be "holy".

One thing is quite clear—and this is found even in Aristotle: if a man is willing to give up his life to attack or kill someone else, it is very difficult and often impossible to stop him. Groups or institutions such as the Secret Service and Scotland Yard are in part designed to prevent the killing of politicians and their families by such suicide bombers. A number of American presidents have been killed by men who did not care for their own lives. But rarely was their motive religious. This power of the man who cares not for his life means, in practice, that if we know someone is on a suicide-bombing mission, he must be stopped or killed first if innocent people are to be protected. The only alternative is to let it happen, because this killing is what the terrorist intends to do and will do, as we see in thousands of instances. Between 9/11 and 2005, there have been 2,400 acts of terrorism in various parts of the world, according to a website that lists them with their times and places.[5] These were from Muslim sources, and they involved the killing of others (but not all were suicide bombings, of course).

The Islamic suicide bomber does not think that those who are killed in his "mission" are "innocent". Subjectively, he

[5] The Religion of Peace, http://www.thereligionofpeace.org.

understands that he is killing "enemies" of Allah, even if those killed are women, children, elderly, or just passersby. This idea stems from a radically erroneous conscience, of course, but it seems to exist. Suicide bombing is rarely random. Someone orders it to happen; someone obeys the order. The purpose of suicide bombers is precisely, by carrying out orders, to help to extend Islam to its "rightful" immediate or long-term dimensions, the conquest of the world for Allah. This great "cause", nutty as it may sound to us, is evidently what gives nobility and dignity to such acts of what the rest of us call "terrorism".

The Erroneous, Deadly Conscience

As I wrote immediately after 9/11,[6] even on the principles of Catholic moral thought—which says that a truly erroneous conscience must be obeyed[7]—it is possible that the suicide bombers went to heaven along with those they killed, if we can assume they were true religious believers and following their consciences with no chance within their culture or personal history of correcting themselves. This view does not make the act right or eliminate its consequences, but it takes seriously what some Muslims evidently hold.

In his encyclical *Veritatis splendor*, John Paul II spent a considerable time discussing the notion of martyrdom. Ironically, that 1993 encyclical was not written with the suicide bombers in mind, though they were already active. The notion of dying for one's faith is an ancient and noble one. It attests to things more important than life. Sometimes, in the course of too many human lives, the only choice available

[6] http://www.tcrnews.com, September 15, 2001.
[7] John Paul II, *Veritatis splendor* (August 6, 1993), 57–64.

was between dying or doing evil. To choose to stay alive
and renounce one's beliefs or understanding of virtue meant
implicitly a denial of the principle at stake. The only way to
uphold the principle in fact would be to accept death, but it
was not one's choice to die as such, hence not suicide. The
tradition—seen in Saint Stephen and Saint Thomas More,
following Christ—was to forgive, but not condone, those
who carried out the death sentence, both the executioners
and those morally responsible for ordering it.

"Charity, in conformity with the radical demands of the
Gospel, can lead the believer to the supreme witness of
martyrdom", wrote John Paul II.[8] He went on, "The relationship between faith and morality shines forth with all
its brilliance in the unconditional respect due to the insis-
tent demands of the personal dignity of every man, demands
protected by those moral norms which prohibit without ex-
ception actions which are intrinsically evil."[9] Among such
actions, the document points out, is "voluntary suicide".[10]
But suicide bombing is something more than just "voluntary suicide". Back in the Vietnam War, we had instances
of Buddhist monks burning themselves to death in protest
against something or other. Though the act was bad enough
in itself, those monks did not intend to take anyone else
with them.

The whole point of the contemporary suicide bomber is
precisely to take someone else with him. And who are these
"someones"? They can be soldiers—usually in areas where
obvious distinctions of combatants and noncombatants is
deliberately obscured. But they can be and often are pas-
sengers in buses or airliners, or shoppers in markets, or just

[8] Ibid., 89.
[9] Ibid., 90.
[10] Ibid., 80.

about anyone. The bombing is of the innocent precisely to make publicity and cause civil unrest and even retribution against some outside the cause.

If the analysis presented here is generally valid, the major conclusion is that any group, religion, philosophy, or world-view that positively advocates and carries out this practice of suicide bombing cannot be true. What is at stake is not merely a distinction between two divergent groups within one religion but the very possibility of any truth existing in that part of the religion that advocates suicide bombing as "martyrdom" in its religious "cause".

4

Nine-Eleven (9/11) Revisited: Five Years Later

I

The fifth anniversary of the wanton destruction of the World Trade Center towers is upon us. We ask ourselves, "Were the three thousand people killed somehow 'legitimate' targets?" and "What was this attack about?" On the accuracy and clarity of our responses everything depends, including the purpose of reason itself. Yet, we are perplexed by the myriad of conflicting and contradictory explanations for the central cause of this day, now called, without further reference, "9/11".

The best anyone can do in these circumstances, it seems, is to provide a solid and well-considered opinion. This is what I shall try to do here. An opinion is an informed judgment based on suitable and available evidence concerning possible actions or explanations. The opinion on which one acts could be wrong, but we always act with some lack of clarity. We are irresponsible in many crucial instances, moreover, if we do not seek to find a plausible and accurate opinion about human events, about what they mean.

Adapted from "9/11 Revisited", *Ignatius Insight*, September 8, 2006, http://www.ignatiusinsight.com/features2006/schall_911rev_sept06.asp.

All human action takes place with partial information. The fear of being wrong in practical affairs is not the beginning of wisdom but the beginning of self-chosen paralysis. As Eric Voegelin said, we need not embrace the errors of our time. Still, we cannot pretend that such errors do not occur; they must be dealt with. Opinions are necessarily the grounds of all political actions, including wars—especially wars. Seldom are things simply black or white. The most we can have is "practical" certainty or judgment, as Aristotle called it. But opinions are not merely vague guesses. At their best, they are based on evidence and experience. They can (and in the case of prudence do) penetrate to the reality that stands midst the flow of other views. Nor, however tempting, are opinions excuses for theoretic skepticism.

The human mind is able to "invent", to use Cicero's word, almost any explanation for some fact or event that really happens. This is, after all, what detective stories are about. The "invention" is the line of reasoning by which we arrive at the intelligibility of what happened. Even when the actors in and the consequences of a deed are fairly well known and sorted out, it is still possible to explain them in different ways. This difference of interpretation should not surprise us. Indeed, after five years there is even a small group of professors—who else?—who insist that 9/11 was an American political plot having nothing to do with Muslims. Almost anything can be imagined if one has a motive.

In the intervening five years, then, we have heard almost every conceivable reason for the attack—except perhaps the best one. When we examine the differing analyses coming from various Islamic sources, from Europe, from professors, from experts, from politicians of widely different persuasions, we cannot but be astonished at the fertility of the human mind in coming to opposite explications for the same event. Without the solid reality of the event itself, we have nothing to check the meanderings of our own minds. All is reduced to irresolvable speculation.

Usually, these alternative explanations will likewise reveal the underlying principles of the individual or the group proposing them. But I do not consider this likelihood to be an argument that everything is subjective. Everyone still claims to be dealing with facts, based on evidence. In this sense, two things exist simultaneously: the knowledge of the facts and the explanation of what we want these facts to mean for our own purposes. Usually, our politics or our philosophy direct us not so much to the facts we see but to the meaning we give to them. Though a few people still maintain that men did not land on the moon several decades ago, no one today maintains that the World Trade Center towers are still standing. I was across the river in New Jersey the other day looking at the Manhattan skyline. The towers are gone. I once was at a Georgetown banquet at the top of one of those towers; the room we were in has just disappeared, but I know I was there. But the fact *that* it is not there does not explain *why* it is not there, nor do most of the whys that we have heard since that time explain it, though most contain some truth or plausibility lest they be not credible at all (however, the theory that it was an American plot deserves no credence at all).

Of course, we know, in another meaning of the word "cause", that the World Trade Center was destroyed because passenger planes, hijacked by young Muslim men who shrewdly prepared themselves just for that purpose, rammed planes into the buildings. We know the physics, as it were, of what happens to such buildings when planes explode against their sides. We are not sure that these men or their instigators were clever enough at building mechanics to have intended precisely the astonishing result they achieved. The plot's stunning success may have surprised even them. In any case, we know that many people in Muslim cities cheered the event as a "success". As far as I know, we have received no apology from those who claim responsibility. They did not warn their intended victims. They were not saddened by their success but content with it. Nor did any one of them offer reparations for the damage they caused. This implies that, in their own minds, what they did was not unjust but an act of virtue. The pilots and their henchmen were, in their own estimation, "martyrs", not "killers".

I argued from the very beginning that the attacks had already begun in the previous two decades with various bombings of ships, embassies, and aircraft in other places throughout the world and that the driving motivation behind them was not secular or political but religious. What was going on came from a theological understanding of Muslim purpose in the world. Even those Muslims, however few or many they be, who did not think that such means were the wisest ones to use nonetheless understood the legitimacy of the purpose behind them.

I further argued that, by not acknowledging this motivation, we in a sense did not do justice to what was going on; we did not, that is, do justice to the men who conceived and carried out the destructive plan. We thus wandered off into fields of explanation that were elaborate, sophisticated, "scientific", and often self-serving but that did not correspond to what we were seeing, to what these men said of themselves. Basically, it seemed to me that by calling this a war on "terrorism", a war against "fanatics" or "madmen", we, in a real way, demeaned both our enemies and ourselves. We did not want to look in the eye of the real storm.

If, on the other hand, we want to call this a "war of civilization", well and good, provided that we realize, following

Christopher Dawson, that civilizations are themselves expressions of religions, or pseudoreligions we now call "ideologies". No civilization in the history of mankind is less amenable to a purely secular explanation of what it does than Islam. Our efforts to explain this war in terms of Western philosophy or science, however elaborate, fail to get at the central issue, the belief that everyone ought to be Muslim, that this is the will of Allah on earth, that there can be no long-term rest until this submission is brought about and "peace" ensues. This motive, invisible to science, is quite visible to those who see it as an abiding mission over time, over centuries. What most handicaps us is an idea that such a purpose cannot abide over time and take various forms of reincarnation, including one in our own day.

II

Let me first run through a number of opinions claiming that the cause of the war is not primarily religion. One view would be that religion is a kind of superstructure dependent on economic issues. Either Islam, because of its own principles, is a cause of economic underdevelopment, or Islamic nations happen to be impoverished because they are the victims of others' greed. Thus, in this quasi-Marxist approach, it is all explained by an economic theory. Islam is not a problem; economics is.

Some sources insisted that the Iraq war was about oil. It is true that oil is the source of enormous Muslim wealth used to finance any expansion effort on its part. Mosques all over Europe and the United States are built and financed by this wealth. But the value of oil has little or nothing to do with economies or inventions that came from Muslim sources.

Even the national land theory that gives a state or a sheik control over certain oil lands is a result of Western political views about private and public property. If one used the theory, sometimes seen in Catholic circles, that the riches of the earth first belong not to those who own the land but to "mankind", we might even deprive these states of the legal right to collect these riches from the land they control.

Another view, that of the famous novelist Salman Rushdie, is that within Islam itself there has arisen a new form of totalitarianism, resembling either Nazism or fascism. Rushdie, along with several other writers and intellectuals, recently signed a manifesto against Islamism that stated, in part, "After having overcome fascism, Nazism, and Stalinism, the world now faces a new totalitarian global threat: Islamism. . . . Like all totalitarianisms, Islamism is nurtured by fears and frustrations."[1] This view admits that a "totalitarian" impulse exists among some Muslims but denies that it comes from anything in Islam itself, either directly or in logic. Thus, those Muslims who claim that what they do is to carry out the will of Allah are in effect heretics, however much they, in turn, claim Rushdie has betrayed Allah in his novels and thus deserves the death that they decree for him.

Canadian columnist David Warren has downplayed the notion that what we are witnessing is a new and improved resurgence of a strong Islam. Islam by every military and economic standard is incapable of any significant military threat. Its rate of real economic growth in all its lands is near the bottom when compared with other nations. Even the explosives used by terrorists are invented and usually manufactured by the West. As a result, Islam is in a state

[1] Quoted in Michelle Malkin, "A Manifesto against Islamism", February 28, 2006, Michelle Malkin's official website, http://michellemalkin.com/2006/02/28/a-manifesto-against-islamism/.

of lethargy. Largely because of its own theories and vices, it cannot definitively act even against weak opponents like those coming from Islamic countries. This view, of course, corresponds with the view of many of Islam's most ardent proponents of violence. They see that the corrupt West is undermining even Muslim values and hence must be destroyed. This theme of moral corruption in the West has many Christian proponents as well, and it contains a good deal of truth.

Scholar Samir Khalil Samir, S.J., takes yet another view. He maintains that the current problem in the Middle East is not religious but political in nature. It goes back to the very foundations of Israel as an independent state after World War II. The Western powers at that time imposed on the Middle East a Jewish state as a kind of conscience payment for their failure to protect the Jews from Hitler. Thus, one injustice was replaced with another. The Islamic world, generally speaking, did not itself have anything to do with Hitler. So the political solution proposed for a Jewish homeland was simultaneously an injustice to Arab peoples already living in that area.

Samir does not deny the legal existence of Israel, which is fully recognized; that situation cannot be changed. What he argues, rather too easily, is that "no war ever accomplishes anything", especially the recent ones. (Does that include World War II? one wonders.) One might recall, in fact, that the reason why most existing Muslim states control the areas over which they rule is that Muslims waged wars that can only be described as "successful" in terms of permanent control. Many of these conquered lands in Africa, Europe, the Middle East, and Asia were once Christian. In the case of Spain, its reconquest of lands taken by prior Muslim invasions of the peninsula seems permanent (or at least did), aside from Spain's current decline in birthrate and influx of Muslim immigrants. The fact is, were it not for two battles, at Tours and Vienna, against invading Muslim forces, all of Europe might well have been Muslim long ago.

In any case, Samir proposes—and it is a good proposal as far as it goes—the establishment of a Middle Eastern Union with international peacekeeping forces together with a basic agreement about common diplomatic principles. He does not concern himself with the earlier history of Islam but begins with the post–World War II situation. He admits it is a kind of "utopian" solution but thinks that it is at least worth trying. The only problem I would have with this proposal is that it does not seem to take into account the corresponding "utopian" motivations of the groups within Islam that we now designate as "terrorists", the very ones who think that what they are doing is carrying out the mission given to Islam by Allah.

Still another opinion is that the so-called terrorists within Islam are a minority. They generally are inspired not by Qur'anic sources but by Western philosophy, especially fascist and Nazi sources. No doubt, again, there is some truth to this. The historic Muslim problem has been its own failure to modernize. The search for scapegoats to explain this failure is part of the drama of modern Islam. One might argue that the problem lies within Muslim thought, but as this approach is unacceptable for many, there must be an effort to use these violent means in the manner of their most successful examples in the last century. This is the so-called Islamofascist interpretation in all its varieties.

Now, all of these views have points that are not to be ignored. Still, even if the most aggressive proponents of recent turmoil admittedly did see the moral weakness of the West to be a major opportunity and many leaders did study in the West, the major explanation is still religious. No doubt, our own internal philosophies—liberalism, multi-culturalism, and ecumenism—militate against elevating religion to such a prominent place wherein it must be dealt with on its own terms. On this premise that the religious explanation is closed, we must look for other reasons. Once we seek to explain our problems in nonreligious terms, we no longer examine the validity of the religious claim on which Islam rests—on its original inspiration, on the texts and the doctrine that is found therein.

Many, no doubt, will be amused if not scandalized by a proposal that suggests that the first principle of practical politics is to take theological positions seriously by examining the validity of what specifically they maintain. By the mere logic of exclusion—seeing as the other explanations do not fully explain—it is really the most sensible approach to the long-range problem that faces us from this source. It is also, paradoxically, the most "ecumenical" view, the one that is willing to take seriously the theological view of those who think that the mission of Islam is to spread the law and worship of Allah to every people. It is not the "moderate" Muslims that we must take seriously but the radical ones.

A central question arises, then, namely: Are there intellectual "tools" available to perform this task? In view of the rather obvious refusal of Islamic sources to have Islam's own doctrine subject to public debate or analysis, one might argue that we should not enter into this sort of discussion. It just creates more turmoil. It is best to stick to those more practical things that we have in common, certain aspects of family values, common economic problems, the price of oil, and so forth.

On the other hand, Islam specifically denies the two basic truths of the Christian faith, the Trinity and the Incarnation, both of which are considered to be in Muslim terms blasphemous. Christians are seen, at best, as polytheists. Except in very restricted instances, Mass or the Bible or any effort to explain Christianity (or other faiths) is not permitted in any existing Muslim state. The civil disabilities that the few Christians in these lands experience are objectively enormous. The literature on how followers of other religions are made second-class citizens within Islamic states is, by any objective standard, conclusive. But these restrictions are the logical consequences of theological positions. It does no good to complain about them unless we are willing at some point to challenge their logical veracity. Indeed, one of the reasons given for not pressing these issues is that doing so would just make it worse for remaining Christians, even costing their lives.

I do not consider that the endeavor to come to terms with what Islam is might be something hostile to Islam or its polity. Indeed, I think the reluctance to come to terms with it over the centuries is one of the causes of the current problems. We really do not have, from the Christian side, any authoritative statement on the question "What is Islam?" It is not enough to speak of "respecting" the followers of other religions without going into what it is they believe and how they practice what they believe. Rather, it is a question of asking, in the most careful and reasonable manner, about the "truth" of what they maintain about themselves. No matter how destructive they are to us, the so-called terrorists—who claim that they do have a religious motive for their deeds—are forcing Christians themselves (and everyone else) to focus on this theoretic core of the problem.

Perhaps the most visible issue that we associate with the resurgence of Islam is, ironically, the use of suicide bombers. No other instrument, I think, could be, from the Muslim terrorist side, more effective than this in giving attention to the seriousness, in their minds, of their cause. We tend to think that a suicide bomber is about as deviant from any understanding of the good as it is possible to get. To arrive at this conclusion, we have to assume that there is such a thing—common to all, Muslim and everyone else—as natural law, or whatever it may be called.

But if natural law itself is not possible in the context of a view of Allah that makes him the arbitrary cause of all activities in the world, with no internal order to either himself or the world, we can have no "natural law". If it is an "insult" to Allah to say that he is not the direct cause of all things, we cannot propose as an alternative the natural law that proposes stable secondary causes that the Muslim will also recognize. The suicide bomber, be it noted, does not see himself as violating any law. In fact, he sees himself as obeying the "law" or "will" of Allah.

We do have instances of Western religious leaders sympathizing with suicide bombers on the grounds that their pain is so great they must lash out. But the "oppression" is usually itself defined in terms of Western political philosophy that no suicide bomber himself would ever follow. Moreover, it seems strange that we do not have the moral passion about this phenomenon that we once heard expressed against nuclear weapons, even now that countries like Iran claim to have a right to them and may in fact have developed them, or are currently developing them.

Yet, I would maintain that it is precisely the matter of the suicide bomber that brings us closest to the religious issue that we must deal with. In terms of the Muslim theology professed by its practitioners, the suicide bombers are in heaven. What they do is wholly justified in religious terms. We cannot simply write this reasoning off as "invincible ignorance". The suicide bomber claims that it is indeed legitimate both to kill himself and to kill innocent civilians in the pursuit of the cause of getting rid of Islam's greatest enemies and eventually establishing the rule of Allah on earth. Suicide bombers are, in their own minds, doing Allah's work.

Again, here I am arguing sympathetically with what the suicide bombers and their promoters think they are doing. I may think, as I do, it horrendous that any mind or religion could come to this view, but some minds and a particular religion have come to this view. If we insist on writing suicide bombers off as mere fanatics, madmen, or hypocrites, well and good. But in so doing, we miss the import of what is going on. We are no longer capable of dealing with the root causes of the problem. Again, the root causes are theological. Basically, the question is whether Islam is true objectively in its explanation of itself. If it is true, why? If not, why not? I think we must locate a place in the culture to begin to treat of this issue in a much more fundamental manner. Dialogue may be good, but it is not the first requirement.

We must be much more aware than we are that Islam denies the validity of the basic truths of what is specifically Christian. We must coldly look at the basis of this claim. Islamic thought explains the Christ phenomenon in such a way that He was not and could not be divine. At most, He was a holy man. To accept this view means that we Christians are required to blaspheme. Moreover, any claim that He was anything more will be considered an insult to Allah. Thus, there are two key questions: What exactly is

Allah, and what is the objective status of this "revelation" that Muhammad is said to have received? Is it in any way credible? When we "respect" other religions, do we imply that the claim for a later revelation that corrected the last Christian revelation is possible or true? And if we deny that it is true, on what grounds? What, in other words, is our argument about these claims as such stated as accurately as possible?

Barry Cooper, in "History and the Holy Koran", the appendix to his *New Political Religions*,[2] has given a survey of those Western scholars, often German, who have gone carefully through the difficult task of tracing the sources of Qur'anic texts, their consistency, age, language, integrity. It is work that often involves much personal danger to such scholars. Publication of such criticism is often considered, like Christian dogma itself, to be blasphemous. Nonetheless, this research and critique, or lack of it, is where the real problem of the war lies. Is it true that Muslim revelation and its proposals are true? If so, the effort to make the world Muslim by such means is justified. Those who think it is true, however many or few, constitute the real origin of contemporary politics in this area.

While I might think that the terrorists have, as they claim, the better part of the argument from within Islamic theology on their own terms, it is up to other Muslim thinkers to prove, again on their own terms, that it does not. But what I think is more fundamental, something that is not really being addressed in any systematic fashion (for a variety of reasons, mostly arising out of our own culture, not out of Islam), is the lack of a serious critique of Islam. We need an examination that is objective, sympathetic, and accurate

[2] Barry Cooper, *New Political Religions; or, An Analysis of Modern Terrorism* (Columbia: University of Missouri Press, 2004).

but one that does not avoid the fact that not a few Muslim thinkers and their political followers think that what they are doing, including acts of terrorism, is nothing less than the will of Allah. It is because we are not willing to face the implications of this more basic issue that we are having so much trouble in the political order. We do not want to name the problem as it is.

Again, what I suggest is an opinion. We should not forget what an opinion is. But it is an opinion, at least in my own mind, that respects Islam for what it claims it is: a religion destined to subject all to the will of Allah. That is why I think its claim, even when principally promoted by what we call "terrorists", needs much more serious intellectual attention than it is receiving. This religious position, accurately spelled out, is, I think, closer than the other explanations to the real cause of that horrific event and day that we know as "9/11".

5

On Politics and Physics: Stanley Jaki on Science in Islam

I

Not since the Crusades, perhaps, has an understanding of Islam's understanding of itself been a more immediate political issue. Behind this sudden rise of Islamic unrest is an issue of deeper import. Stanley Jaki has been one of the few scholars knowledgeable enough and careful enough to address the origins of the problem that lies behind the public unrest. At bottom the issue is nothing less than Islam's understanding of the meaning and nature of its God, of Allah. The other and more visible civil turmoils are the consequences, carried out in different ways, of the implications of this basic issue.

Bernard Lewis, in his Jefferson Lecture of 1990, saw the issue in terms of "secularism and modernism", which presumably could be relied upon to tame this Islamic turbulence. He said, "The war against modernity is . . . directed against the whole process of change that has taken place in the Islamic world in the last century or more and has

Adapted from "On Politics and Physics: Stanley Jaki on Science in Islam", *Fellowship of Catholic Scholars Quarterly* 32 (Summer 2009): 14–17, https://www.catholicscholars.org/PDFFiles/v32n2sum2009.pdf.

transformed the political, economic, social, and even cultural structures of Muslim countries."

Islamic fundamentalism has given an aim and a form to this otherwise aimless and formless "resentment and anger of the Muslim masses at the forces that have disrupted their societies . . . robbed them of their beliefs, their aspirations, their dignity, and, to an increasing extent, even their livelihoods."[1] Jaki's position addresses the very origins of this modernization and secularization in a unique way because he sees the centrality of science and religion in these very changes while at the same time he rejects the secular humanist implications that seem to be present in Lewis.

William F. Buckley Jr., likewise, has taken note of the perplexity we have in understanding Islamic aims and principles: "We are, after all, face-to-face with something very different from the religion common to our own culture." In Islam, the law as put forth in scripture (the Qur'an) and tradition (the Sunnah) is "to be reflected exactly not only in the personal lives of believers, but also in the laws of the state as well. . . . The government of Muslim states is explicitly an institution of God."[2] It is this understanding of law that deserves some further attention, in the light of Stanley Jaki's work.

An abiding theme in the work of Stanley Jaki concerns the various stillborn historic initiatives to begin science and to sustain, once begun, its self-generating progress. We might like to believe, perhaps, for cultural or ecumenical reasons,

[1] Bernard Lewis, "Western Civilization: A View from the East" (Nineteenth Jefferson Lecture in the Humanities, Washington, D.C., May 2, 1990), 23.

[2] William F. Buckley Jr., "Unfamiliar Foe among Us", *Washington Times*, July 8, 1993, G3.

that science could have commenced anywhere, at any time, with any people, with any cultural, religious, or philosophic presuppositions. The fact is, however, that science requires certain definite habits of mind, certain understandings about the reality of the world, and certain epistemological ideas about the relation of mind and reality.

Without these specific ideas and habits, moreover, there will be no original or continuing science. To be sure, any human being, in any time or place, can in principle learn and understand such principles and habits we call science if he has the will, the talent, and the understanding to do so. That too is part of the very meaning of both universal science and universal human nature. It is only in this latter sense of a common human nature in a real world that we can know with our given intellects that a universal philosophy and an abiding truth open to all men are possible.

In the history of the world, it was neither necessary nor inevitable that science would develop in the first place. And by changing our ideas, it is still possible for it to disappear even where it has already materialized. In those places in the world where science has not appeared, furthermore, it will not appear or develop until certain and known ideas and basic views of the world are accepted. All these observations should be stated with the full realization that some scientists can be charlatans, while many errors are found in the very effort to develop science, the importance and meaning of which errors Stanley Jaki has himself clarified in a magnificent passage in *The Relevance of Physics*.[3]

---

[3] Stanley Jaki, *The Relevance of Physics* (Chicago: University of Chicago Press, 1966), 219–21.

II

Readers of Jaki's work are familiar with his discussions of the fate of science in China, Greece, India, and Mexico, as well as in Islamic countries. Unlike many historical discussions of the origins of science, Jaki's work takes seriously the specific differences of beliefs, customs, and philosophies as reasons for the origin and the continuation of science or the lack thereof. Jaki is objective enough to grant that certain ideas are necessary for certain developments to take place. Not everything can come from anything. Some ideas, some theories, some experiments, and some endeavors just will not work without the idea that truth is the conformity between mind and reality.

In the case of Islam, in particular, Jaki argues that the notion of Allah as pure will found in the Muslim theologians and philosophers makes science, in principle, impossible.

What is occurring in the Muslim world today is a confrontation . . . between a very specific God and science which is a very specific antagonist of that God: the Allah of the Koran, in whom the will wholly dominates the intellect. A thousand years ago the great Muslim mystics al-Ashari and al-Ghazzali denounced natural laws, the very objectives of science, as a blasphemous constraint upon the free will of Allah. Today, the impossibility of making ends meet without science forces the Muslim world to reconsider its notion of Allah.[4]

---

[4] Stanley Jaki, "On Whose Side Is History?", in *Chance or Reality and Other Essays* (Lanham, Md.: University Press of America; Intercollegiate Studies Institute, 1986), 242.

Jaki thus sees that the real problem, even with science, is theological. An all-powerful God free even from the principle of contradiction makes the meaning both of God and of the created world impossible to ascertain. On this premise, science as an investigation of and knowledge of a reality that is simply given, but given to be what it is, becomes impossible.

On the surface of things, however, this position—that science investigates a real, finite world to find its universal laws that can be discovered and formulated by the human mind—might seem perfectly obvious were it not for the cultural and theoretical issues involved. Both the conflicting claims to truth of the various religions and the claims to the unknowability of truth in relativism and multiculturalism make it seem that science itself as a claim to truth is a very limited, even dangerous, thing.

If science is a good thing, however, and if it bears a true description of an actual world in all its interrelationships, then ideas—religious, philosophical, racial, or cultural—that do not allow for this scientific understanding must in some sense be not merely unworkable but positively wrong. If and to the degree that there is a scientific truth, positions contradictory to it, which cannot in principle support its premises, cannot be maintained except at the cost of making science subjective (Kantianism) or of giving up science altogether—which a people, a nation, a religion, or a culture is free to do.

What is most countercultural in Jaki's own work, of course, is his argument, made with great care and erudition, that at the origins of science as we know it lie certain theological positions that deal with the actual world, particularly those of the Creation and the Incarnation.[5] The question of the relationship between reason and revelation arose

[5] See Stanley L. Jaki, *Universe and Creed* (Milwaukee: Marquette University Press, 1992).

because of the historic confrontation of Greek science and philosophy with the three established revelational religions.[6] Primarily, this is an issue in Judaism, Islam, and Christianity, though in some respects Plato is pertinent here also.

The most important question that arises, consequently, concerns the relation of Judaism, Christianity, and Islam to science and its origins. This issue is particularly pertinent since it has been claimed all through modernity that science undermined religion. Jaki's work is precisely to examine the tenuous basis of this claim, without denying the problems science causes religion. The case of Islam falls under this general consideration as an example of a religious theory that cannot, in principle, maintain the logic of science and simultaneously be consistent with itself.

Jaki argues that the origin of modern science is medieval, that the first law of motion was a medieval discovery (Buridan). Jaki further argues that this law was originally formulated because the theological position of Christianity on creation from nothing required the rejection of a pantheist or animist view of the world, especially a rejection of the notion of the eternity of motion. Motion thus had to have an initial impetus or cause. Jaki further argues that the doctrine of the Incarnation of Christ was the doctrine that forced attention to the specificity of the world in time and of each moment and being in it. In general, science could not develop without the notion of a beginning in time in which, however, there were stable secondary causes that had their

___

[6] See Étienne Gilson, *Reason and Revelation in the Middle Ages* (New York: Scribner's, 1938); James V. Schall, *Reason, Revelation, and the Foundations of Political Philosophy* (Baton Rouge: Louisiana State University Press, 1987); *Faith and Political Philosophy: The Correspondence between Leo Strauss and Eric Voegelin, 1934–1964*, ed. Peter Emberley and Barry Cooper (University Park, Pa.: Pennsylvania State University Press, 1993). Jaki's own most thorough treatment of these issues is in *The Road of Science and the Ways to God* (Chicago: University of Chicago Press, 1978).

own reality, nature, and stability. Science was an account of specific events, specific relationships that were observed, tested, understood.

III

With this background, Jaki has a particular problem with Judaism, Islam, and Eastern Christianity, each of which would, paradoxically, grant the doctrine of the Creation of the world. Eastern Christianity, moreover, would have no difficulty with the Incarnation; but science did not originate there either. Thus, in Jaki's argument, there must be some teaching or doctrine in Western Christianity that was particularly apt for the beginnings and progress of science. This was the doctrine of creation from nothing that caused Buridan to realize that motion must have a beginning and not be eternal, that once begun, motion would not stop unless impeded by something outside of itself.

Jaki, of course, does not deny the basic Christian teaching that neither the Creation nor the Incarnation can be proved by science, though he does hold that the existence of God can be proved from reason through the finite things that exist. Jaki, in agreement with Aquinas, does not hold that either the doctrine of the Creation or the doctrine of the Incarnation can be the conclusion of a scientific premise, however much they are not capable of being shown to be contradictory to any truly scientific position.

Jaki's position is more subtle, more attuned both to the nature of reason and the meaning of revelation. In his work on Duhem, we find, for example, the following passage: "In a footnote [F.] Mentré felt it important to warn against what he termed an already widespread misinterpretation of Duhem's thought: 'Duhem does not say that modern science is a product of Christianity; he rather says that Christianity has been an auxiliary, and an indispensable one, to the scientific development.' "[7] In his footnote to this passage, Jaki comments briefly, "This is an all-important point, often forgotten in sympathetic portrayals of the role of Christianity in the rise of science."[8]

What was Jaki's problem with Islam's notion of God? At the end of his essay "The Physics of Impetus and the Impetus of the Koran", Jaki wrote:

> The whole question of why science was not born within the Muslim milieu, or the question of why the physics of impetus was not formulated there, is in the end a theological question, which can only be answered in terms of theology, such as the true nature of the Koran's impetus. The significance of this result will not seem minor at a time when religious revival is at work in the Muslim world with a greater impetus than perhaps ever before in its history.[9]

Clearly, in Jaki's analysis, some aspect of Allah, as described in the Qur'an, makes the ability properly to see science impossible, whereas there is something in the Christian understanding of God the Creator that fosters this relationship.

What is the essence of Jaki's position? Briefly, that the orderly notion of science—the three laws of motion and the engineering that developed as a result of these laws—required a proper view of the actual world and what happened within it. The crucial Muslim thinker is Avicenna (d. 1037). The Qur'an did have a notion of the Creation, but

[7] Stanley L. Jaki, *Uneasy Genius: The Life and Work of Pierre Duhem* (The Hague: Martinus Nijhoff, 1984), 231–32.

[8] Ibid., 232n36.

[9] Stanley Jaki, "The Physics of Impetus and the Impetus of the Koran", in *The Absolute beneath the Relative, and Other Essays* (Lanham, Md.: University Press of America, 1988), 151.

Avicenna held a Plotinian emanationism in which creation of new beings from nothing is replaced by a transformation of God Himself into everything else. God eternally produces the world, but He is not a Creator.[10] Like the Latin Averroists, Avicenna and the Arab philosophers put Aristotle's pantheism ahead of the Qur'an.

The Muslim philosophers held a kind of two-truth theory to protect both themselves and the Qur'an. They opposed, by using uncritically Aristotle the philosopher, the more conservative Muslim view of Allah. This conservative view to exalt God or Allah was forced logically to an occasionalist position. Occasionalism denied, in the name of the power of God, any real causality in secondary natures in the world. Thus, if God could create, it was apparently a greater power for Him to create every moment than if He left other beings their own power to act. Muslim orthodoxy "rejected the notion of scientific law for fear that it would impose constraints on the infinite power of Allah, the Creator".[11]

Since Muslim scholars failed to formulate a proper idea of creation from nothing in time from a definite beginning, Jaki concludes that this failure is a theological failure. It results in either occasionalism or pantheism, neither of which can found science. Jaki further analyzes the position that science is merely a result of civic development with no need for religious or philosophic ideas to support it. The two-truth tradition that proposed to let the two spheres exist side by side with no attempt to relate one to the other left the culture and the philosopher at war with each other and with no firm basis for science in either system.[12]

[10] Ibid., 146–47.
[11] Ibid., 147.
[12] Ibid., 148–49.

Jaki points out that the exposure of the Muslim world to science and technology has made it alert to its own inferiority in the area of science. No theory of exploitation or military submission confronts the real problem, which is the absence of an understanding of the world and its causes, including the nature of God and creation from nothing, which makes science possible. Essentially, Jaki is arguing that a religious and philosophic consistency of idea and action would in fact result in a true representation of God and the world, one that in fact has been worked out in the history of science. In this context, it would be wrong to consider Jaki either as anti-Muslim or pro-Christian; rather, he should be viewed as someone who sees where the issues lie and who is willing to spell them out and articulate their relation to a true understanding of science and its history.

"The Muslim world is fully justified both in deploring the abuses of science and in trying to apply science in a humane way", Jaki concluded with much sympathy.

> But before that humane application takes place, there has to be science, that is, there have to be minds fully familiar with science. This view, however, demands that there be minds fully imbued with the thinking underlying science especially if they wish to be creative in science. The question is then whether the present-day Muslim reawakening, which is a reassertion of the role of the Koran in every facet of life, can be reconciled with the thinking demanded by science.[13]

Clearly, on the basis of the Muslim theoretic understanding of Allah and of the consequences of that understanding of the world and its laws, Jaki does not think the impetus of the Qur'an is compatible with the impetus of science.

[13] Ibid., 148.

Neither wars nor acrimony will resolve the validity or invalidity of this position, only the accurate and true understanding of both the theoretic positions of the Qur'an and of science. Eventually, true ideas must replace untrue ones. No religion or philosophy or science would, in Jaki's view, have it otherwise if such principles are clearly spelled out. Jaki's service to Islam is of a piece with his service to Judaism, Christianity, and science itself, a persistent, clear presentation of what science is, what religion is, and how they might relate to one another.

6

The Ambiguity of Islam

Many books on the meaning and the apparently sudden rise of Islam have been published since September 11, 2001. For overall insight, it is still difficult to surpass Belloc's chapter "The Great and Enduring Heresy of Mohammed" in his 1938 book *Great Heresies*. But books such as Laurent Murawiec's *The Mind of Jihad*, Reza Aslan's *No God but God*, Roger Scruton's *The West and the Rest*, Tawfik Hamid's *Inside Jihad*, Matthias Küntzel's *Jihad and Jew-Hatred*, and Bat Ye'or's *Eurabia* are a few of the newer books that are making an important contribution.

Several books on this pressing topic are especially of interest to Catholics: Jacques Jomier's *The Bible and the Qur'an*, Daniel Ali and Robert Spencer's *Inside Islam: A Guide for Catholics; 100 Questions and Answers*, Thomas Madden's *A Concise History of the Crusades*, and, most recently, Samir Khalil Samir's *111 Questions on Islam*, a book originally written in Italian. My own *Regensburg Lecture* is also pertinent here.

It is the Samir book about which I wish to comment. Father Samir is an Egyptian Jesuit, an adviser in the Holy

Adapted from "The Ambiguity of Islam", *Homiletic and Pastoral Review*, November 1, 2009, http://hprweb.com/2009/11/the-ambiguity-of-islam/.

See, with roots in Cairo, Beirut, and Rome. An essay of
his in the *Asia News* is entitled "When Civilizations Meet:
How Joseph Ratzinger Sees Islam". In it, Samir writes:

> Benedict XVI has stated more exactly the vision of John
> Paul II. For the previous pope, dialogue with Islam needed
> to be open to collaboration on everything, even in prayer.
> Benedict is aiming at more essential points: theology is
> not what counts, at least not in this stage of history; what
> counts is the fact that Islam is the religion that is develop-
> ing more and is becoming more and more a danger for the
> West and the world. The danger is not Islam in general, but
> in a certain vision of Islam that does never openly renounce
> violence and generates terrorism, fanaticism. On the other
> hand, he does not want to reduce Islam to a social-political
> phenomenon. The Pope has profoundly understood the
> ambiguity of Islam, which is both one and the other, which
> at times plays on one or the other front.[1]

Samir's comments on Islam are often the best around.

Samir calls himself "culturally" an Arab, but religiously or
theologically a Christian. Samir is learned in the language,
the literature, the folkways, and the philosophy of Islam. His
book contains a glossary of Arabic terms and its own useful bibliography. This book is a must-read for anyone who
sees the need to understand what Islam is about, something
to be avoided only at the price of political and theological
blindness. What Islam is about is no longer a kind of ro-
mantic reflection on a stagnant culture. Today it is a very
aggressive religion whose reaches affect not only who lives
next door to you, but the price of gas, the ownership of
banks, the need for and the size of armies, and the accurate
understanding of one's own faith.

---

[1] Samir Khalil Samir, "When Civilizations Meet: How Joseph Ratzinger
Sees Islam", *Asia News*, April 2006.

This book is written by a man who is both sympathetic toward and critical of Islam. Samir knows its philosophical and theological backgrounds, as well as its history from its appearance in the seventh century on the Arabian peninsula. The book's presentation is frank—Samir pulls no punches —but its author never speaks without accurate knowledge and clear conviction.

The question-and-answer format of the book works well. The questions cover most of the basic issues, from suicide bombing to the status of women to the Muslim understanding of Christianity. Yet, I found the book rather frightening in its honest and direct presentation of what Islam does, holds, and seeks, of what it does when it conquers, and of the intensity of its beliefs, which in so many ways are so ill founded. Basically, if it could, Islam would convert the world, one way or another, by peace or by war, as precisely the "will" of Allah. It really has little place for anything else, except when Islam cannot prevent its presence.

We really have no idea what we are up against unless we take a careful look at what is held theologically and what has happened historically in the Muslim world and its understanding of the world outside itself, which it calls the sphere of war. The voluntarism of Islamic thought enables it, apparently, to justify means of advancement that are by any reasonable or democratic standard immoral. Indeed, as Benedict noted in his Regensburg lecture, this voluntarism and its invalidity stands at the intellectual root of Islam's self-understanding.

Many Western writers on Islam today, especially in explaining its violence, want to interpret this violence as somehow an aspect of Western ideology, as if there were no roots of it in the sources of Islamic revelation itself. It is true that a number of modern Muslim thinkers were influenced by

Lenin, Marx, or other revolutionary thinkers. There is a modern component. But there was violence in Islam's expansion from its beginning.

Islam aggressively conquered large areas of the world, often ones ruled by unprepared Christians. Its methods of rule by tribute, second-class citizenship of the conquered, and isolation of subject groups are grim to contemplate. Much revolutionary Muslim theory and practice would want to rid Muslim lands of all foreigners who do not accept the Qur'an and its law. To a large extent, the exodus of non-Muslims from Muslim-controlled lands is happening. The Holy See has often sought to stem this tide, but one can hardly blame Christians and others from leaving such hostile environments while there is still time and still someplace to escape to.

The solution to the problem of Islamic violence, according to these same contemporary thinkers, is to "Westernize" or "modernize" Islam—that is, make it something other than it conceives itself to be. While there may be some of this secularizing that is feasible—to "democratize" Islam—the drift is now decidedly in the other direction after the independence of Muslim states after both wars. Muslim states are under pressure of their own religious enthusiasm to reject overtures to modernity as contrary to Islam.

The advantage of Samir's book is that he sticks to Muslim history and practice. He gives the most sympathetic interpretation of Islam that is possible based on the evidence. But this is a man with no illusions. He is not without some hope, but still, no illusions. He understands that many Muslims look at the West not as a haven of good living but as a morally corrupt, decadent society. Hence, to them, the notion of Western superiority is absurd. We do not judge Islam by its standards, and it does not judge us by our standards. Islam does not have a tradition of natural law in the ordinary sense that would signify a rationale that all men could accept apart from their religion.

Most people today in the West are covert multiculturalists. They assume that Islam, Christianity, Judaism, and the rest of the religions believe in the "same" God by different expressions. When we dig a little deeper, however, we run into Chesterton's remark that most religions are alike in their rites and external garb, but they differ in what they believe God to be. Here, in fact, they differ vastly. We are used to hearing that we all believe in the same God, but investigation makes this view tenuous.

The French scholar Sylvain Gouguenheim, in pointing out that Aquinas did not get his knowledge of Aristotle solely from Arab texts, says this of the Muslim understanding of Allah:

> To proclaim that Christians and Muslims have the same God, and to hold to that, believing thereby that one has brought the debate to its term, denotes only a superficial approach. Their Gods do not partake in the same discourse, do not put forward the same values, do not propose for humanity the same destiny and do not concern themselves with the same manner of political and legal organization in human society. The comparative reading of the Gospel and the Koran by itself demonstrates that the two universes are unalike. From Christ, who refuses to punish the adulterous woman by stoning, one turns to see Mohammed ordering, in the same circumstances, the putting to death of the unfaithful woman. One cannot follow Jesus and Mohammed.[2]

Samir also uncovers the tenuousness of the thesis that the God Allah and the God of Christ are the same God.

[2] *Brussels Journal*, January 5, 2009.

The Qur'an specifically denies the two basic elements of the Christian notion of God. Both the Jew and the Muslim agree in rejecting the God who is Trinity and one of whose Persons became man. For those not prepared to accept the Qur'an's bluntness, the most surprising thing is what it says about Christianity. Samir is very good here. He is careful to point out that the Church has never said that Muhammad was a prophet. Moreover, for the Muslim, Christ is not the Son of God but a prophet, important but by no means superior to Muhammad, whose status as the last prophet enables him to explain Christianity's unique doctrines simply as heresies or errors.

Both the Trinity and the Incarnation are scandals to the Muslim mind. Originally, it is held, everyone was Muslim. The whole of Genesis is rewritten, including the sacrifice of Isaac. Everyone is "naturally" Muslim. The "natural law" of human beings is not some rational understanding after the manner of Aristotle but the law of the Qur'an. This law, for the true Muslim believer, should eventually replace all existing laws in modern states.

Samir explains why a Muslim rejects the Trinity. The Muslim thinks the doctrine means the existence of three gods, an error that did not begin with Muhammad. The notion of three Persons in one God seems too subtle. The Muslim rejects the Incarnation because there can be only one God. God cannot "generate", contrary to the Christian Scriptures and their understanding of generation within the Godhead. Muslim monotheism is absolute. No room is left for a Word made flesh, let alone a Son and Spirit within the Godhead.

The attraction of Islam, it is often said, is its relative simplicity. All that is required is to follow the five obligations: faith in Allah and his prophet Muhammad, praying five times a day, almsgiving, fasting, and the pilgrimage to Mecca. By comparison, Christianity demands a philosophical thought that does not simply reject the Trinity as three gods or the Incarnation as a degradation of God into matter. Simplicity of practice is not a virtue when it comes to the proper understanding of revelation.

One of the most useful things that Samir does in this book is to explain how the Muslim will understand us. He will see signs of weakness in what we call simple goodwill or cooperation. We see the suicide bomber as a kind of blind madness or fanaticism. Samir explains how Muslim theologians have worked around suicide bombing so as to justify it. The suicide bomber even becomes a "martyr". In this case, suicide bombing becomes a kind of personal sacrifice, even though many others are killed and suicide was generally condemned in Muslim tradition.

Samir is aware that many Muslims just want to live in peace. But others have a much more aggressive concept of what Islam is about. They think that everyone should be Muslim. A Muslim who converts to another religion or philosophy can be subject to death. Muslim countries will vary in how this penalty is carried out, but it is a factor that is not simply imaginary.

The people of the world, to worship Allah properly, should all be subject to Islamic law, which should be enforced by what we call the state. Samir recounts that in Islam there is no real distinction between state, religion, and custom. There is absoluteness in this worship that allows no one to be outside. Jews and Christians, as a sort of compromise, are given a certain second-class status in Muslim countries, provided they pay a tax and do not seek to convert Muslims. Those who are not Jews or Christians technically can be killed. It is difficult to believe that such rules or traditions exist, but they do. And they are not seen as in any way wrong. They are part of a pious effort to subject all things to Allah.

In short, the "III questions" of the title of this very incisive book are designed to ask every question one may have had since Islam forced itself before our daily attention. Again, Father Samir is both a hardheaded and a sympathetic critic of Islam in all its phases. The book has much force to it precisely because it is written by someone who has been in immediate contact with Islam all his life. He has studied the texts and the history. But he also knows both Christianity and what we call the modern state. The book is often as hard-hitting about the West as it is about Islam.

When one has finished this book, he sees the Muslim with clearer eyes. The whole history of Muslim philosophy is a valiant attempt to make sense of the Qur'an and its practices. It does not think that anything is lacking in the Qur'an, which is said to be divinely transcribed. Efforts to examine the literary and historical sources of this text are much too rare and indeed can be dangerous.

The notion of a modern, progressive, technological society is not particularly in the forefront of the pious Muslim's mind. The irony, of course, is that it is precisely this modern technology and its relation to oil that has supplied the Muslim world with the cash to become much more aggressive.

Samir's discussion of why the mosque is not a church and of why the Saudis are involved in spending their oil riches, not to help the poor, but to build mosques all over the world, while at the same time forbidding the presence of Christian churches in their own lands, is most sobering. Considerably more people are converted to Islam each day than are converted from Islam. The great political fact of our time is the increasing presence of Muslims in Western lands that managed in previous eras—at Tours and Vienna —to prevent Islam from taking over Europe at a much earlier date.

Over a fifth of the world's population is Muslim. In many ways, most of the military hot spots in the world today have something to do with Islam. Its nature and its presence cannot be ignored. How does one think of this? Samir's presentation of Benedict XVI's view is quite to the point. It is practically impossible to have a theological discussion with Islam. In the first place, there is no Muslim pope. There are many centers and sources of the interpretation of its law. Not all agree with each other on basic points. Benedict seeks to find a minimum basis of conversation, not so much of high theology, but of ordinary decency. There must be an explicit rejection of the use of violence as an act that has religious sanction.

This incisive book deserves widespread reading. It is clear, sensible, and well informed. It represents what the service of intelligence to the faith really means. It follows Aquinas' dictum that we must understand a position urged against the truth. Only in understanding this can we estimate what we are up against and begin to think of how to confront it. Father Samir's *111 Questions* will do more than start us thinking about these issues. It will lay out the whole scope of what the "ambiguity of Islam" means.

7

A Jihadist Conquest?

What follows is an opinion. An opinion means that, of two sides of a contradictory proposition, both sides have evidence, neither conclusive. The proposition I address, and it needs frank address, is this: *Those active, believing, and armed Muslims who hold that Islam must set forth to conquer the remaining world for Allah, whatever this faction's relative size, not only have the better side of the argument about whether the Qur'an and actual Muslim history support them but have, in the next half century, if persistent, a high probability of success.* The contradictory opinion is: *Islam is peaceful and, in any case, has no chance so to prevail.*

For what it is worth, though many recent books support the latter contention (list on request), objectively, the first proposition is better supported by the evidence, and the faction mentioned therein is acting, as we speak. Do not be scandalized if Schall and bin Laden agree on this view of Islam. These militant representatives, who to us are mere "terrorists", do intend to conquer the rest of the world for Allah, as he commanded them to do. Progress is being made.

Adapted from "A Jihadist Conquest?", *Catholic Thing*, November 2, 2010, https://www.thecatholicthing.org/2010/11/02/a-jihadist-conquest/.

This mission will not be stopped unless made to stop. I do hope for, but do not count on, another Tours or Lepanto—military defeats terrorists plan to avenge. The jihadist mind is shrewd. It reads Western cultural and moral decline as indicating Islam's own "historic moment", which, as Belloc said at the end of *The Crusades*, offers it the chance to do exactly as it did before.

While much cynicism and corruption are found among the jihadists, a genuine motive we call "religious" is evident. That is why most of our sociologists and philosophers cannot get a handle on it. Scientific methodology excludes the spiritual. We really do have "martyrs" who, in the name of Allah's reign, seriatim blow themselves up with tens to thousands of innocent people (who they think are "guilty"). Islamic theologians tell Muslims that the perpetrators, as a result of such "noble" deeds, are in heaven. Many Muslims believe them.

This interpretation, that it is legitimate to kill the innocent to expand Allah's reign, is one of two "nuclear bombs" the Muslim world possesses. The first is its relative population increase and the Western world's decrease. The second is the suicide bomber universalized. This is why Benedict XVI made a point about the latter in his Regensburg lecture. Philosophic voluntarism that justifies violence has to be confronted head-on. When the suicide bomber detonates his explosives, he is more lethal than anything Iran is developing. The suicide bomber can blow himself up anytime, anyplace in the world, among the small or the great. His potential for civil disruption in world cities is almost infinite, once widely put into effect. Jihadist theorists know this potential. Our unused atom bombs worry us. The randomly exploding pipe bomb is intended to terrify us.

Samir Khalil Samir, the authoritative Egyptian Jesuit, in

his book *111 Questions on Islam* concludes precisely that in the Qur'an it is possible to discover good evidence for both of these propositions: *Holy war is justified* and *Holy war is not justified*. The jihadists are not deranged for finding support for holy war there; nor are those uninformed who do not find support. I conclude from this that those whom we designate as "terrorists"—designated as such so that we do not have to face the issue of whether what they propose follows from their religious beliefs—are faithful to the Qur'an and to Muslim history. That history also recalls the arms that conquered much of the Islamic world as we now know it, much of it formerly Christian lands held by those who would not or could not prevent the conquest.

I am quite prepared to analyze Islamic power in terms of the Aristotelian category of regimes. In structure and practice, most actual Muslim regimes are monarchic or tyrannical in rule. I doubt, however, that the legal structure of these states, whose boundaries were often drawn by European colonial powers, is particularly effective for the more recent across-all-borders awakening of Islam to the possibility of world conquest. Nor do I think some Machiavellian, Leninist, or Nietzschean "will to power", rather than religious belief, is what is primarily behind it all. The religious belief that the world *should* be subjected to Allah and his law under a universal caliphate is what is operative. World conquest in praise of Allah is an idea, almost unfathomable to us, that has lasted down the centuries since Muhammad's blinding military career.

I am somewhat sympathetic to this Muslim project to complete what is considered to be the mission of Islam in the world, that all be subject to Allah. I think it is a contorted version of "Go forth and teach all nations." Both the understanding of God and the means are different. That is the problem. We do not want to face it. The jihadists do.

8

On the Fragility of Islam

Islam is the longest-lasting, closed, unchanging socioreligious culture to appear among men. Its very idea is that everyone worships Allah over time in the same way, with the same simple doctrine. The major change Islam looks to is not modernization or objective truth but, in a stable world, the submission to Allah of all men under a caliphate wherein no nonbelievers are found.

We still look back at communism, at least the Western variety, with some astonishment in this regard. Almost no one thought it could "fall" without a major military encounter. That it disintegrated so quickly and so completely seems incomprehensible to anyone but a John Paul II. He understood its frailty, its failure to understand the human soul and its origins.

Islam is far older than Marxism. In the seventh century of our era, Islam appeared suddenly almost out of nowhere. It rapidly spread, mostly by military conquest. Its immediate victims were the Byzantine Christian lands and the Persian Empire. Both proved incapable of rising to their own defense. Islamic armies eventually conquered North Africa,

Adapted from "On the Fragility of Islam", *Catholic Thing*, August 23, 2011, https://www.thecatholicthing.org/2011/08/23/on-the-fragility-of-islam/.

the Mediterranean islands, much of Spain, the Balkans, the Near East, the vast land area from southern Russia to India and Afghanistan, and even parts of China. Indonesia was a more commercial conquest.

Later efforts of Europe to regain some of these conquered lands worked for a while. The Crusades ultimately failed, though they indirectly prevented further Muslim conquest of the rest of Europe. Spain, Greece, and parts of the Balkans managed to regain their lands. But the control of the Muslim lands by European powers in the eighteenth and nineteenth centuries made little real inroads into Islam itself. Islam was exposed to Western power and science, but that did not effect any significant inner conversion, except perhaps to create Muslim confusion about its own lack of science and technology.

The Muslim conversion of former Christian lands seems to be permanent. What few Christians are left in these lands are second-class citizens. They are under severe pressure to convert or emigrate. Many forces within Islam desire a complete enclosure of Islam that would exclude any foreign power or religion. The Muslim world is divided into the area of peace and the area of war; the latter is what Islam does not yet control.

So with this background, why talk of the "fragility" of Islam? This instability arises from the status of the text of the Qur'an as a historical document. The Qur'an is said to have been dictated directly in Arabic by Allah. It has, as it were, no prehistory, even though it did not come into existence until a century or so after Muhammad.

Scholars, mostly German, have been working quietly for many decades to produce a critical edition of the Qur'an that takes into consideration its prehistory. Due to the Muslim belief that any effort to question the Qur'an's text is blasphemy, the enterprise is fraught with personal risk to the researchers. The idea that the text cannot be investigated, of course, only feeds suspicion that even Muslims worry about its integrity.

Much of the philosophy within Islam, as we know, had roots in scholars who were originally Christian or Persian. This is well recorded in Robert Reilly's *The Closing of the Muslim Mind*. But even more, the Qur'an itself seems to be composed of many elements from Christian or Hebrew Scripture. The very word "Qur'an" has roots in liturgical books.

The systematic denial in the Qur'an itself of the Trinity and the Incarnation, the reducing of Christ from the Messiah to another prophet, force us to inquire about the connection between the Qur'an and the Judeo-Christian Scriptures. The broader claim that Muhammad's "revelation" rewrote and made obsolete the earlier revelation needs direct confrontation.

The interfaith movement has limited its relations to Islam pretty much to areas of mutual agreement. This is well enough. But one cannot ignore the issue of truth about a text and the grounds on which it is based.

Religion or faith, even in Islam through Averroës, has been conceived as a myth designed to keep the people quiet. The scholars could quietly let the caliphs and the imams rule if the intelligentsia were left free to pursue philosophy, which was conceived to be anti-Qur'anic in the sense that the Qur'an did not hold up under scrutiny about its claims.

The fragility of Islam, as I see it, lies in a sudden realization of the ambiguity of the text of the Qur'an. Is it what it claims to be? Islam is weak militarily. It is strong in social cohesion, often using severe moral and physical sanctions. But the grounding and the unity of its basic document are highly suspect. Once this becomes clear, Islam may be as fragile as communism.

9

On Rereading Regensburg

The "Regensburg lecture" was delivered by Benedict XVI on Tuesday, September 12, 2006, five years after 9/11.[1] It was an academic lecture, one of the greatest in that genre ever given. It was delivered in a forum familiar to him, a place where, though the world was looking on, he could still assume that he would be understood, with all the nuances, freedom, and implicit suppositions that went into the scholarship behind the lecture. In reading the lecture, one could feel the warmth and affection that the pope had for his German academic experiences.

The immediate reaction to the lecture was not unlike that given to Alexander Solzhenitsyn after his Harvard lecture of 1978, and in a way for the same reason. It showed again the relative separation from politics and publicity that academia requires if it is to be able to speak the truth of things, a truth

---

Adapted from "On Rereading Regensburg", *Vital Speeches of the Day* 72, no. 25 (2007): 706–10, lecture delivered to Fellowship of Catholic Scholars Conference, Washington, D.C., September 29, 2012.

[1] Benedict XVI, lecture, University of Regensburg, Germany, September 12, 2006, 19. Text in James V. Schall, *The Regensburg Lecture* (South Bend, Ind.: St. Augustine's, 2007), 130–48. References to the Regensburg lecture will be given in parentheses in the text.

that academics themselves do not always welcome. This latter topic, to speak and to understand the truth of things, was the purpose and the justification of a university as such. The lecture also showed the intellectual courage that is often required to speak the truth in any modern forum, especially an academic one. Ironically, academia itself sometimes requires police and military protection for it to be what it is intended to be. The pope recognized this fact of reality (13).

If anything was particularly frightening about this lecture, it was the threat of violence that it brought forth and the reasons for it. Little doubt remains that this threat is on the minds of all university lecturers and researchers that seek to discuss the truth, especially of Islam and of modern relativism. Universities themselves do not include all truth, conspicuously that of revelation, within their sphere of interest. The last sentences of the lecture are these: "It is to this great *logos*, to this breadth of reason that we invite our partners in the dialogue of culture. To rediscover it constantly is the great task of the university" (63). The Regensburg lecture is nothing less than an effort to reestablish among us, or establish for the first time, as the case may be, just what a university is in its entirety, and what it is to deal with—that is, everything, including revelation.

The Regensburg lecture is the first important papal document in modern times that addresses in any way, in the light of its record, the question "What is Islam?"—a question that is itself at least fourteen hundred years old and still lacks a thorough and official treatment in the light of Christian revelation, the two basic points of which, the Trinity and the Incarnation, Islam specifically denies. Yet, in addressing this question in the way he did, through the logical consequences of theological voluntarism, Benedict detected the same issue in Western philosophic and scientific presuppositions that are fundamental to explaining Islam's rationale about itself. Eastern and Latin Averroism curiously resonate with each other. Looked at in this light, the lecture saw what few others were willing to see: namely, that what separates Islam and modern thought is not so distant after all. Actually, the recent rise of Islam is possible because in various ways, many Muslim politicians and thinkers see this inner coherence between them.

In this sense, I think, Benedict was more immediately interested in the soul and mind of the West than that of Islam, which latter, in its premises, has remained pretty much fixed for centuries. Finding some way to "talk" with Islam has been on the agenda for some time. The initiative, the forum, and even the idea of a forum, usually come from the side of the Church with roots going back to Plato and Aristotle. Islam, perhaps sensitive to the implications of its own philosophical roots, does not really seem interested in talking to anyone except on its own terms. A resurgent, confident, and aggressive Islam is a problem of major political proportions. But little is new about this issue, except the confidence. The worldwide expansion of Islam so that all the world would be subject to Allah was part of its original inspiration.

What is remarkable, however, is that Islam and modern secular science and politics may well be intellectually closer to each other than either is to classical philosophy and Christian revelation. This philosophic closeness is what the Regensburg lecture was about. The two-truth theory in Islam meant that Allah could change his mind, and hence reality, on any question so that nothing in reality was stable. Hence, it could not be examined by reason. Truth could be contradictory; otherwise, Allah's power was said to be "limited". In the West, in a logical development that led from Scotus to Hume, once any trace of order in nature was removed, the human mind could make reality into whatever it wanted it to be. Both positions held that nothing necessary or stable could be found in God, man, or nature. The divine mind of Allah and the human mind of the relativist scientist ironically were identical.

The Regensburg lecture is a remarkable example of putting things together, always itself a basic purpose of intellect. In a relatively short lecture of some fifteen pages, many apparently diverse and disparate things are related to each other in a coherent, logical way. The pope is a master of the philosophical whole. In the citation above, Benedict makes the provocative point that the encounter of Greek thought and revelation was not a matter of chance.

Most historians of philosophy, of course, will maintain that it was merely an accidental encounter or else one of necessity. And from a human view, they may well be correct except for one thing. It is not merely a question of scientific theory and a possible philosophy of history. The pope implies that it was neither mere chance nor absolute necessity, both of which have a proper place in the reality that does exist. At some level, the encounter and its results were intended. If this is so, what was the purpose of the encounter between what have come to be called Jerusalem and Athens?

I

The starting point of Benedict's reflection is Paul's call to "come over to Macedonia" (Acts 16:9). Many philosophers of history have worried about or ridiculed the idea that God chose a certain obscure tribe in the Middle East in which initially to reveal His purpose. "How odd of God to choose the Jews!" was Belloc's amusing remark. The pope implies further that, Paul's being sent to Macedonia—that is, to Greece, to the land of the philosophers—implies that he was *not* being sent to, say, India, Japan, Africa, China, or any other religion or culture, at least in the beginning. Before this farther sending could happen, the encounter with Greece first had to take place. Paul was being sent among the philosophers, whom he would meet, unsatisfactorily, in Corinth, Athens, and Philippi, whom he would sometimes even call "foolish" (1 Cor 1:20). Evidently, something was found developed in Greece that was not seen so well elsewhere. This uniqueness of Greece would have something to do with the "multiculturalism" that the pope saw as the third and perhaps most dangerous step in the process of dehellenization that followed from the rejection of the proper relation of reason and revelation.

Benedict, however, does not find it at all odd that God chose the Jews. In the Old Testament itself the Jews are not exactly praised for their good qualities of steadfastness to Yahweh. They often seem fickle, complaining, and unfaithful to the terms of their divine selection. Looking back at the Old Testament from Macedonia, however, what does Benedict see? He sees that, in the Hebrew Bible, we already find certain philosophic intimations that pointed to Greece, that is, to philosophy.

We are used to the notion that revelation is something, as it were, beyond reason. Philosophy cannot directly conclude to revelation. But we now begin to wonder if revelation is rather something directed to reason and that this relation was among the first things that had to be worked out in the early Church. The "I am" of Exodus and Christ's oft-repeated "I am" take on a considerably new light when read against the works of Plato and Aristotle.

Benedict concludes from this relationship that the going

to Macedonia was not just an accident; rather, it was intended that revelation be first addressed to philosophy, not to religion. What is understood by this relationship is far-reaching. It meant that all knowledge is not to be based on revelation. Reason has its own scope and approach that need to be set in motion precisely to see that revelation is addressed to it. "John thus spoke the final word on the Biblical concept of God, and in this word all the other toilsome and tortuous threads of Biblical truth find their culmination and synthesis. In the beginning was the *logos*, and the *logos* is God, says the Evangelist" (18).

This passage recalls the *Confessions*, where Augustine describes his first encounter with the Platonists. There, he tells us, he did find the Word (the *logos*), but he did not find that "the Word was made flesh." If man's own reason could on its own power conclude that God was Word, it follows that there was not one single method wherein we were to come to a knowledge of the truth. Or to put it another way, the two ways seemed to belong to each other, to complete each other, to indicate that both arose from the same source. Faith was not "irrational". It was addressed to a reason already operative in things that were discoverable by the human intellect (23).

Benedict sees in this relationship the origin of Manuel II's awareness that God does not approve of violence or irrationality (24). The Byzantine emperor belonged to that assimilation of Greek philosophy and Christian revelation that understood that certain acts were against reason and therefore against the will of God, against His *logos* (23). This combination is what in fact formed Europe (30). It also meant that Europe was something more than a geographical area. It was a place where this encounter of reason and revelation was possible (29).

Benedict contrasts this position with that of Ibn Hazm,

a medieval Muslim theologian. "Ibn Hazm went so far to state that God is not bound even by his own word, and that nothing would oblige him to reveal the truth to us. Were it God's will, we would even have to practice idolatry" (15). This view, developed further by al-Ghazali and other Muslim thinkers, is the central idea, whether it be Muslim or otherwise, that concerns Benedict.

II

After discussing this classic and medieval background, Benedict turns to modern times. He tells us that almost immediately after the clarity of the relationship of reason and revelation was established, particularly with Aquinas, it began to fall apart. The "falling apart" is in effect the separation of reason and revelation, but it is also a denial of reason. The pope traces this process in three steps of what he calls "dehellenization". The first step took place with the Reformation (33-34). The Reformers thought that there was too much metaphysics and philosophy in Catholicism. They wanted to return to faith that did not see itself obliged to account for reason.

The second step had to do with Kant. He separated reason and faith entirely, so that they did not relate to each other. After this separation, he sought to save them both. Faith was concerned, not with theoretical intellect, but only with practical intellect. How we lived was not related to what we knew. He denied faith access "to reality as a whole" (35).

Harnack took up this position, somewhat following Pascal's distinction between the god of the philosophers and the God of Abraham. Harnack wanted to make faith the object of modern science. Thus, he wanted to reintroduce it into the universities. How to do this? This move makes Christ merely a fine man. He has no divine overtones. We study Him as we would study any historical figure. The divine in Him is simply dropped, not considered itself a source of knowledge about His being (37). Jesus was a "moral" model, not an object of "worship" (38). Christ became a "humanitarian".

Christianity was "liberated" from metaphysics and theology. What was left? Christ was not divine. Christianity was purely "historical". Therefore, it could be readmitted into the university (39). Here again Benedict sees Kant. Modern reason limits itself to only what it can find by its own methods. "The modern concept of reason is based . . . on a synthesis between Platonism (Cartesianism) and empiricism, a synthesis confirmed by the success of technology" (40). The Platonic element is the mathematical side of matter. The assumption is that mathematics reflects an objective structure in matter. The formulae of mathematics actually work to deal with material things. Modern science thus presupposes quantity. Nature can also be used for human purposes so that the method of verification and falsification is used (42).

III

It is from this background that the modern notion of certainty comes, from mathematics and empirical verification. Soon this approach would mean that all human and social sciences also had to conform to this theoretic presupposition. Benedict then points out that this methodology in its very presuppositions excludes God and all the really human things that make life meaningful (46). Clearly, theology cannot be considered as "scientific" from these premises. Yet, if science is to be a "whole", if it is to include everything, it cannot exclude "the specifically human questions about our origin and destiny" (48). These questions are still raised by religion and philosophy. All that is left by this method is a "subjective" conscience with supposedly no objective correspondent.

From this approach, ethics and religion lose their community-forming basis. Everyone has his own view of things. Things do not form something on which we can objectively agree. The pope sees this as a dangerous situation because ethics then seeks to base itself on some ideology, not on reality, in order to keep people together (49). The notion that a community is held together by a common understanding of the good is eliminated.

This background brings Benedict to the third stage of dehellenization. This is the modern "multicultural" or "diversity" stage. To arrive at it, we again return to the Scriptures. The hypothesis is that no intrinsic reason exists why Christianity went to Greece, to philosophy. Paul could have turned any direction. This position means that we must take out all the Greek influences in the faith. We must then direct our attention to other cultures, whatever they are, to become part of them (50–51). We cannot ask of them the question of reason.

Benedict does not think this view is "simply false". Some good is found in every culture. The New Testament was written in Greek, and there were Old Testament overtones (52). Not all elements of the early Church needed to be preserved. Which ones should be is why we have a Church and why the Church also needs reason. In a most significant passage, Benedict adds, "The fundamental decisions made about the relationship between faith and the use of human reason are part of the faith itself, they are developments consonant with the nature of faith itself" (53). This reasoning is why the pope does not say that Greek philosophy is simply Greek. The basis in *logos* is what lies behind the concern about the voluntarism in Islam and other religions. The going forth to baptize and teach all nations carried with it a position on the validity of reason in any culture.

Benedict emphatically denies that his position is a rejection of what is valuable in the modern age. "The positive aspects of modernity are to be acknowledged unreservedly" (54). Yet, mind, including the modern mind, is to be "obedient to truth" (55). It is necessary also to see the dangers that lie in modern science. To do this we must bring reason and faith together again in a new synthesis (56).

Theology belongs to the university, not just as a quaint historical study, but as a discipline that asks questions about the whole beyond the self-limitation of scientific methods. But this exclusion is a prejudice of our positivism. The rest of the world sees that human questions must be asked about God and what it all means. "A reason which is deaf to the divine and which relegates religion into the realm of subjectivism is incapable of entering into the dialogue of cultures" (58).

With that passage, Benedict turns the whole issue of multiculturalism around. At the same time, he addresses all cultures from the basis of reason, the universal reason that was met by the initial thinkers of Christianity. He does not allow them a "culture" that denies or ignores reason. The same is true of the self-limiting of a scientific method that claims to deal with the truth by leaving out most of man's really important questions.

Here Benedict, as he often does, returns to Plato. He tells us that this Platonic element in our civilization "points beyond itself and beyond the possibilities of its methodology"

(59). What does Benedict mean by this? He means that, if there is a mathematical structure to matter, it did not put itself there. The discovery of the order of nature leads not to skepticism but to a kind of substitute reason that does not explain itself. Such questions can be "remanded" by the sciences to philosophy and theology. Philosophy is a source of real knowledge (60).

At this point, Benedict recalls a striking passage from Plato's *Phaedo*. It is addressed to the question of many false philosophies that abound. The implication is that nothing true can be found in their midst. What is true is seen as just another falsity. And there are many false theories. This attitude leads to the position that nothing can be true.

Socrates' response to this situation, something Benedict agrees with, is this: "It would be easily understood if someone became so annoyed at all these false notions that for the rest of his life he despised and mocked all talk about being—but in this way he would be deprived of the truth of existence and would suffer a great loss" (61).[2] The fact of a multiplicity of error is not a proof that no truth exists.

The aversion to considering this full scale of truth has "endangered" the West, with its own roots in *logos*. We need the "courage" to open ourselves to "the whole breadth of reason". "A theology grounded in Biblical faith does address itself to the reason that is found in things" (62). This interrelation of faith and reason was forged when Paul was called to Macedonia. The going forth to baptize and teach all nations was itself in divine providence contingent on this first meeting of Jerusalem and Athens.

Benedict ends his lecture by citing Manuel II: "Not to act reasonably, not to act with *logos*, is contrary to the nature of

----

[2] Benedict is quoting Plato, *Phaedo* 90c–d.

God." This affirmation arose from the emperor's "Christian" understanding of God. Both Islam and the universities are invited to the great *logos*, to the "breadth of reason" (63). The final words of the pope are that such is "the great task of the university". In this sense, from the background of the nature and the history of voluntarism, we are left to wonder whether in fact we actually have many universities among us.

10

On "Dialoguing" with Islam

The world today sees a sudden aggressive presence of Islam in a way not seen since the defense of Vienna in 1532. Large numbers of Muslims are now aggressively present in the West and on all Islam's world borders. They insist on retaining their religion and customs wherever they reside. They present internal problems in Western nations that they have not had to face before. The leading forces in Islam seem to have decided that the best way to expand through and defeat the West is not by imitating modern science and technology but by establishing and enforcing Muslim law everywhere, either gradually or quickly.

Yet, a hardheaded Muslim intellectual today, if there be such, would have a sense of the history of theology and of the military means by which Muslim expansion originally took place. He might well judge that everything seems to be falling into place. Two dangerous "technical" developments could undermine Islam's present rigid hold on its own people and its recently renewed determination to expand. A long-dormant Islam, but one that lost few follow-

Adapted from "Dialoguing with Islam", *MercatorNet*, July 1, 2014, https://www.mercatornet.com/articles/view/dialoguing_with_islam.

ers in the five centuries since it lost world political power, has overcome its inferiority complex with regard to Western modernity. It has, in various ways, symbolized by the bombing of the World Trade Center by primitive means, developed a new way to defeat advanced technical power that is no longer morally confident of its own principles.

The first caution to this advancement thesis is the realization that vast undeveloped quantities of oil and gas are known to exist outside of Islamic borders. These rapidly developing resources, plus several significant nuclear energy advances, might well, if used with political shrewdness, make Arab oil considerably less important and profitable to the world economy. Arab power and religious expansion have been fueled by oil money. But little in the Arab world itself was the cause of these oil-based riches. Islam sat on oil, protected by Western theories of sovereignty, but it did not develop the economy or the tools that made oil valuable. Much of Arab oil wealth, moreover, has gone into the private hands of rulers and their families. Arab countries themselves are quite poor and comparatively backward.

The second threat to Islam stems from studies, especially in Germany, of the technical background and actual history of the Qur'an, a study forbidden in Islam itself, probably out of fear of these very findings. The claim is that the Arabic Qur'an came directly from an eternity next to Allah. It was given to Muhammad. It had no prehistory on earth.

Such views cannot be reconciled with variant Qur'anic texts, many of which were deliberately suppressed. The Qur'an was never subject to the methods of scientific criticism. The work on a critical edition of the Qur'an promises to show that the Qur'an is not what it claims to be. It had prior texts that were later woven together in a fashion that revealed internal contradictions in the Qur'an itself. It was out of these latter contradictions that the philosophic theories of voluntarism arose as the only way to defend what the Qur'an actually said. The crisis will occur when Muslims finally understand that the Qur'an cannot possibly be what it claims to be. And this claim rests on clearly examined grounds that anyone can understand.

But while these two approaches are well advanced and foreshadow serious crises in Islamic culture and politics, an even more basic issue is that of the philosophic suppositions on which Islam has had to base itself in order even to imply that its revelation made sense. Few have looked into this background more acutely than Robert Reilly. His book *The Closing of the Muslim Mind* presents his basic arguments and the grounds for them.

However, here I want to comment on a more recent and shorter booklet that Reilly has written assessing the possibilities of any meaningful dialogues between Catholics and Muslims. Reilly's reading of Muslim texts and arguments in this area are wide-ranging. I will not here attempt to reproduce them. His presentation of what Muslim authors say and do is clear in any reading of *The Prospects and Perils of Catholic-Muslim Dialogue*.

What I wish rather to do is to summarize the issues themselves. Reilly argued effectively in *The Closing of the Muslim Mind* what he here restates. A school of Muslim thinkers, the Mu'tazilites, did accept the validity of the Greek notion of reason. This acceptance was something that Christianity itself did almost from its very beginning when Paul was called to Macedonia. A later school of Muslim thought, that of the Ash'arites, whose major figure was al-Ghazali (d. 1111), rejected any relationship between the Qur'an and human or divine reason. This school became the main school of Islamic thought. It dominated almost all Muslim thinking. It is this background that Reilly presents so effectively.

How Much Do Christians and
Muslims Have in Common?

The context of Reilly's analysis is based on Catholic efforts to enter dialogues with Islam about their acknowledged areas of agreement and disagreement. The initiative for these conversations is almost never from the Muslim side. Some attention was paid to Islam by French and German thinkers as by Belloc in the 1900s.

But it was Vatican Council II and subsequent Catholic initiatives to converse with Islamic leaders that set the stage for Reilly's analysis. Catholics often assumed and stated that Islam and Catholicism had many things in common. At first sight, they all believed in justice and love, they wanted peace and disliked war, they believed in the one God of Abraham, and they respected each other's religion. So it seemed sensible to spell out in further detail their disagreements in the light of common principles or words on which both sides could agree.

It turned out not to be so simple. The single most significant reason for this inability to come to agreeable terms is rooted in the philosophical presuppositions that Islam chose to accept if it was, in its own eyes and those of others, to be consistent with itself. In case after case, Reilly shows that Catholic-Muslim dialogue fails or is dangerous because Muslims usually know exactly what they mean in their own theoretic terms, while many Catholic participants tend to assume that words have the same meaning in Islam as in the Western tradition.

If a Muslim and a Catholic agree that they should work for "peace", for example, the Catholic means by this word simply a condition of nonwar or nonviolence. By true "peace", however, the Muslim means a world in which everyone is Muslim. Less than that, we have a state of war between the

Muslim seekers of "peace" and those who are not yet Muslim. It is important to realize that the Muslim is not necessarily seeking to trick the Catholic here if the Catholic has not gone to the trouble to know what Muslims mean by "peace" and "war". Muslims understand "dialogue" to be a practical means to further Muslim goals of a world at "peace" where everyone worships Allah. Those who do not accept this understanding are seen to be in opposition to Islam.

Obstacles to Dialogue

Reilly argues that Benedict XVI, in his Regensburg lecture and other comments on Islam, is one of the few thinkers who really grasped what is at stake here. He understood that no dialogue of any sort could exist between Islam and Catholicism so long as Islam completely "dehellenized" itself, that is, so long as it rejected reason as based in God and in nature. Benedict also realized that because of the resulting emphasis on a will-based understanding of God, many strands of Western thought were converging to the same philosophic conclusion, namely, that no order could be found in nature.

The one flaw in the Reilly book, I think, is that the author does not point out that the Hobbesian understanding of rights and the Muslim understanding of the power in Allah have the same intellectual presuppositions. Only if we give an account of rights that is completely different from that which is mainly operative in modern philosophy can we argue that Islam ought to accept the rational basis of human rights. Human rights in the West have become themselves a relativism whereby any "right" that the individual or state decides is such, is, on that basis alone, a human right, however much it may be opposed to what Catholics call "natural law".

Benedict thought that there might be a few social or moral issues on which Muslims and Catholics could agree, but that until Islam formally rejected the notion that Allah can do whatever he wants, including the opposite of what he said before, no real dialogue with Islam would be possible. Pope Benedict insisted that the Muslim world needs to reject violence as contrary to God's *logos*, or reason. It had to affirm and enforce within its borders a religious freedom that did not mean Islam's "right" to use violence in the name of Allah or give second-class status to non-Muslims. Both sides had to agree that what is unreasonable cannot be maintained. For a Muslim, the notion of reason, whereby God can prohibit what is unreasonable, is said to limit the power of Allah. Hence, to claim the primacy of reason in God is blasphemy because it denies God the "power" of contradicting Himself.

The "freedom" of Allah is such that he can will the opposite of what he willed yesterday. He can command violence to propagate Islam without contradiction because no contradiction is possible. This issue is what Benedict was getting at in the Regensburg lecture when he cited the Muslim theologian Ibn Hazm, who affirmed precisely this "power" in Allah. In this context, as Rémi Brague has recently observed in his book *On the God of the Christians (and on One or Two Others)*, it is very difficult to identify what "God" means to Christians with what Muslims mean by "Allah". So long as this radical difference is not recognized, real understanding between Muslims and Catholics is impossible.

In the history of Islam, we see a continual use of force. Originally, Islam expanded by conquest of Christian lands, which, except for Spain and the Balkans, it was never forced to give up. Once a land is Muslim, it must remain Muslim. Moreover, force can be used to expand religion and to prevent Muslims from changing their religion. Indeed, originally, everyone was said to be Muslim, including Adam. If someone was not Muslim, it was because some parent or body interfered. By right, everyone is and should be Muslim.

If a Muslim suicide bomber dies while killing others, he is considered to be a martyr of the faith. By dying trying to terrorize unbelievers, he shows his piety. Christians and Jews are said to be treated with a special tolerance because they believe in the Book. This special treatment means, in practice, that they are second-class citizens who must pay a special tax. They can have no real part in the public order. No Christian or Jewish books or symbols are allowed. This arrangement is considered to be just, or even kind. Islam has no real notion of citizenship or civic equality or freedom. The mosque is not separated from the state. The state is an instrument in the expansion and the protection of Islam. The state and the mosque operate together, even though, at times, military rulers prevent extremes. At the price of death, no Muslim can convert to another religion.

A fascinating section of Reilly's essay concerns the careful manner in which Muslim apologists deal with the "One" that is Allah. The Qur'an specifically denies as possible the Trinity, a life of otherness within the one Godhead, and the Incarnation of one of its Persons. These positions are contrary to the oneness of Allah. No distinctions of reason or theology are allowed. Moreover, the Bible itself is said to be corrupted. Abraham was originally a Muslim. Muhammad came to rewrite Scripture so that these Christian blasphemies against Allah could be removed. While Jesus is said to be a prophet (something Islam shares with modern liberalism) and Mary a holy lady, nothing divine hovers about them. Thus, it is quite difficult to see how a dialogue could take place when the very thing that needs to be discussed is denied and said to be blasphemy.

The Basic Principles of Reality

All of this background leads to the Muslim need of a voluntaristic metaphysics if there is hope of making Islam seem anything other than utterly incoherent. Basically, its "logic" ended up accepting the incoherence in the name of emphasizing Allah's complete power and man's complete powerlessness. This view leaves to man only the obligation of complete submission to Allah. The purpose of Muslim jihad is ultimately to accomplish this worldwide submission, which is claimed to be the will of Allah. And it is not complete until everyone else makes this same submission. If no reason or order is found in Allah, this means that we can find no secondary causes in ourselves or in things. Nothing follows from anything.

In the end, Reilly points out that no such a thing as "authority" exists in Islam. We do find, out of the limelight, certain Muslims who understand their civilization's backwardness and the incoherence of voluntarism. The need for the "rehellenization" of both Islam and the West ironically comes to a head at the same time. In insisting that Allah can do the opposite of what he did yesterday, in allowing violence as permitted by Allah's will, Islam is very close to the modern liberal democratic position that we can have a "right" to what is against reason. What counts is only what Allah or the Leviathan wills.

What is at stake in the Muslim-Catholic dialogue, which

this essay of Robert Reilly makes vividly clear, is the importance of understanding that God is *logos*, that what is created in His image follows from this understanding of God. When God or nature becomes simply will, everything is permitted to reach our end, whether it be a utopia or a world submissive to Allah. Reilly supplies, in clear terms, what has long been lacking, a straightforward explanation of why Muslim and Catholic dialogues achieve very little. It is because, when Muslims and Catholics do manage to understand each other, they cannot agree on the basic principles of reality.

11

"Try to Understand": Mosul

The Italian journal *Corriere della Sera* published on August 9, 2014, the statement of the exiled Chaldean archeparch of Mosul, Amel Nona. The statement is brief and exceedingly powerful. Christians have been in Mosul for seventeen hundred years. They are driven out or killed by the new Islamic State following the principles of its own founding.

We think that these tragic events do not affect us. Archbishop Nona does not agree. "Our sufferings are the prelude of those you, Europeans and Western Christians, will also suffer in the near future. I lost my diocese. The physical setting of my apostolate has been occupied by Islamic radicals who want us converted or dead. But my community is still alive." This blunt passage is not unlike that of the archbishop of Chicago, who has stated that he expects his successors either to be jailed or killed.

Such events make us realize how difficult it is for us to understand something like the killings of Christians in Mosul and other Muslim places. We like to think we can get

---

Adapted from "A Chilling Warning to the West from the Archeparch of Mosul", *Aleteia*, August 19, 2014, http://aleteia.org/2014/08/19/a-chilling-warning-to-the-west-from-the-archeparch-of-mosul/.

along with everyone, that these are deeds of "fanatics". It cannot happen here. But we can no longer be so sure of this. It turns out that our constitutional and sentimental views almost make us blind, not to the event but to its causes.

"Try to understand us", Archbishop Nona pleads. "Your liberal and democratic principles are worth nothing here." Indeed, we can even argue that these principles paralyze us and make us blind to the reality of persecution by and in Islamic spheres. "You must reconsider our reality in the Middle East because you are welcoming in your countries an ever growing number of Muslims." We think these immigrants are coming to find jobs or to escape violence. But in fact many are coming with missionary purposes, to convert in one way or another everyone to Islam. The Christians of Mosul were given the standard Muslim choice—conversion or death. Some managed to flee. The Islamic State means business.

"Also you are in danger. You must take strong and courageous decisions even at the cost of contradicting your principles." We wonder: What is the man saying? Contradict our principles? Are these principles not what make us free? The archbishop sees them as the avenues by which the Islam that is now destroying his diocese and city will destroy European and American cities. We find this preposterous. Hence, we will not consider that the archbishop may well be right. This is just some religious aberration in some far-off place.

We are largely utopians who think that things are as we want them to be. We are not realists like a man becomes who sees his people killed and the physical buildings of his people either destroyed or taken over. Is the archbishop wrong to universalize his experience? Is this not just a passing local affair? "You think all men are equal, but that is not true.

Islam does not say that all men are equal. Your values are not their values. If you do not understand this soon enough, you will become the victims of the enemy you have welcomed in your homes."

The Muslims who immigrate into Europe or America often do not assimilate. They soon form their own enclaves wherein they can practice their own religion under their own law. This phenomenon is what the archbishop was pointing to. The clash of values is a momentous one, but it is a clash of values, a completely different understanding of what man, God, and the world are about.

The archbishop's message to us is a warning. But it will not be believed. He seems to be aware of this. His witness is disturbing enough because it brings to our attention the plight of his people. But it is even more disturbing as an understanding of our culture and values from the outside. It is not that Islam is unintelligible. Rather, it is unintelligible if we persist on seeing it through our principles, which are not universally accepted when we assume they are. "Try to understand" this fact. Such is the last message from Mosul's Christian martyrs.

12

The Islamic State

I

An Islamic state is one that officially declares itself to be governed by the strict rules of Islamic law. Within it, no non-Muslim or what is judged to be a blasphemous presence is allowed. This internal purity is understood to be the proper submission of mankind to the will of Allah. A caliphate is the rule of an imam or leader, preferably of the house of Muhammad, chosen by Allah, to rule all the Muslim faithful (*ummah*). A caliph, however chosen, is deemed to be a successor to Muhammad to carry out his mission of conquest and conversion.

The historic caliphates, such as that of the Ottoman Turks, which lasted to the end of World War I, only partly succeeded and eventually disappeared, of course. But Islam does not eschew patient conquest one step at a time. Once a land is conquered by Islam, it is considered forever to be part of Islam, even if, as in the case of Spain, it is expelled from its first conquest.

The presently declared Islamic State, with its caliph, exists in parts of Iraq and Syria. It is a beginning. Can this caliphate, with the help of newer jihadist movements such

---

Previously unpublished. Written in September 2014.

as Hamas, al-Qaida, and the Muslim Brotherhood, expand to incorporate the many other Muslim states? This result remains to be seen. The Islamic State's leaders, because of certain cultural and religious changes in the West that they see as a decline in morals and will, think that it is time to try the next step, which is to expand into Europe and America. Only China, Russia, India, and parts of Africa remain. Aggressive Islamic movements are found within or on the fringes of each of these areas.

The revival of Islam is certainly the most significant world movement since the collapse of communism. Though Islam has been in the world since the seventh century and, in a few centuries, conquered a fifth of the world's land and population, we know more about short-lived communism than we do about long-lasting Islam. Both of these movements had visions of world conquest—both can probably be best understood as perverted and tortured interpretations of Christ's admonition to go forth and teach all nations.

II

If only to see it spelled out clearly, I want to argue here a minority opinion: namely, that those who hold that everyone in the world should be Muslim and brought under Muslim law by fear, force, or choice are the most authentic and logical Muslims. They are the ones that can best lay claim to interpret and carry out the Qur'an correctly. Or, perhaps better, since the Qur'an contains contradictory positions on many topics, the proponents of Islamic State can assure themselves that their view is certainly in conformity with the Qur'an. The voluntarist idea that rules Muslim thinking holds that Allah can make one thing true one day and its opposite true the next. To deny Allah this paradoxical power would be to limit an all-powerful deity superior to the distinction between good and evil.

In addition, Muslim legal opinion holds that statements appearing later in time in the Qur'an or in its official interpretation replace earlier statements in the Qur'an that seem to limit Allah. All of these legal and philosophical positions imply, as I see it, that the Islamic State, using whatever means it thinks needed or useful, including mass killings of Christians and other minorities, can claim full subjection to Allah's will. No matter how atrocious such means appear outside of Islam, they do have legitimate justification within the Muslim mind. Critical ideas of such procedures are simply not allowed within the Islamic State. They would be seen as blasphemous. The choice of conversion, second-class citizenship, or death, given to people who are not Muslims, is considered to be just and according to Muslim law.

Within Islam there will always arise those who can correctly claim that this universal conquest of the world in the name of Allah and the cleansing of non-Muslims is what Islam requires as a religious duty. Forces within Islam may at times settle for less, or the whole Islamic world, as in the sixteenth to the twentieth century, may have to retract because of the superior strength of its enemies. But this subjection, step by step or all at once, of the world remains its justification and goal. It is understood to be the will of Allah found in the Qur'an, with which no compromise is possible.

Such unity of unwavering purpose throughout the centuries seems strange, though there is a certain nobility to it. The real question has to do with the end, not the means that seem like raw violence to the outside world. If the Islamic State's understanding of Allah is true, then what it does needs no further justification. If we do not face the question of the truth of Islam and the validity of its claims in its own terms, the force of Islam will go on, as it has, century after century, until it finally succeeds in its world conquest. Islam is a system that thinks it has covered all the objections to it. It sees our time as ripe for long-delayed action.

Of course, looked at through Western eyes, or Hindu eyes, or almost any non-Muslim's eyes, those who hold this position of world conquest are classified as "fanatics" or "terrorists". These terms are largely those of Western political experience applied to Islam. But they deftly avoid facing just what real Islam is all about. Liberal ideas about diversity, free speech, and democracy with conservative ideas about human worth prevent an accurate evaluation of what these ideas of conquest mean. They do form the heart of Islam as a religion. In itself, Islam does not carefully distinguish between religion and politics. I do not think that advocates of an Islamic state are, as we like to call them, Islamic "heretics" or adherents of some sort of modern ideology. Some Islamic thinkers are influenced by Lenin or Hitler, but not as their primary inspiration.

Rather, with some exceptions, advocates of the Islamic State are Muslims who faithfully follow what this religion allows and encourages them to do. These are the true believers. To look on them in any other way is not to do them justice or honor. To look on them as heretics or aberrations results in policies that only make the Islamic State's success more likely.

The Muslim notion of a division of the world between that of war and that of peace can only instigate the effort to eliminate the world at war (the non-Muslim world) so that all can live in Islamic peace where no non-Muslim presence exists. When a Muslim speaks of "peace", he means a world in submission to Allah. The notion of dealing with such a movement in terms of "dialogue" simply will not work for philosophic reasons that should be obvious. Muslims of a true Islamic state do not dialogue except, when forced, to their own advantage, when other means are not at hand. If we say that this view does not "respect" the Muslim religion, the only answer seems to be that it is the only view that does respect the religion for what it claims itself to be.

III

History and geography have given us many different Muslim states. There are military dictatorships that see their function to moderate the extremism of the true believers and clergy. There are absolute monarchies. From British and French rule there are parliamentary forms, though all are subject to and acknowledge Muslim goals. While all Islamic states have much in common, the Islamic states that we see in the Middle East vary from Indian Muslims to those in Indonesia.

Muslim immigration has made Islam's presence increasingly felt in the old democracies. Usually Muslims do not integrate into the culture that they enter. This refusal is itself part of the religion. Converts from Islam, if there are any, are often killed or threatened with death. Most European countries have large Muslim conclaves that are largely closed to outsiders. Population growth in Muslim areas causes some Muslim thinkers to speculate on a "democratic" takeover of many European countries in a few decades. This eventuality will not necessitate outright war but will entail the same results. Once Muslims are in power, however achieved, Muslim law can be put into effect and enforced.

If anything is clear, it is that, contrary to their beliefs, Muslims fight among themselves. The Sunni-Shiite warfare is much observed. Islam looks for a way to transcend this division to present again a united front to the world. This unification seems to be what the new Islamic State thinks it is about. But real Islam knows that it is destined to conquer the world in the name of Allah. We find it difficult to think that such a goal could abide over centuries. But if we look at the history of the rise of Islam, the religion was from the beginning a successful military operation against usually Christian armies that were not well enough prepared, either intellectually or militarily, to stop this expansion.

With some major exceptions, such as Indonesia, the expansion of Islam was due first to military conquest, then gradual conversion. A few minorities of non-Muslims—the Copts in Egypt, the Chaldeans in Iraq, the Christians in the Holy Land, the Jews in several places—remained as small enclaves with second-class citizenship within the Muslim state. As in postmedieval Europe, the very word "state" indicated an entity over and above the people to rule them. Many modern Islamic boundaries were established by European powers during the colonial era to democratize them. The Islamic State strives to supplant this alien system.

Though some Islamic states, notably Iran, threaten to become nuclear powers, it is safe to say that Muslim armies as such do not present a threat to most of the world in terms of modern arms. However, what Islam learned, or thought it learned, from 9/11 and other such murderous initiatives is that terrorist and city warfare from within can disrupt and undermine any sophisticated modern state, no matter how many advanced arms it possesses. It is this combination of true belief in world conquest and the means of justified terror that we see happening all over the world. Older Muslim states that were monarchies or military dictatorships gave some stability but still second-class citizenship to non-Muslims. These compromised Islamic states see themselves threatened by the tenets of the new Islamic State, which seeks first to conquer from within all Muslim states into one caliphate.

IV

As I say, this analysis seems to me to be the proper understanding of the Islamic State coming into existence. A 2014 essay in the *American Thinker* went through, century by century, the number of people killed by the expansion and wars of Islam. It comes to about 250 million. "Unlike the 20th-century totalitarians whose killing fury consumed themselves, reducing their longevity, Islam paces itself. In the end, though slower, Islam has killed and tortured far more than any other creed, religious or secular." Like many authors who write of Islam's actual record, this writer did not identify himself by his real name—he is "an American who is not Jewish, Latin, or Arab".[1] The Muslim apologist of the Islamic State may or may not confirm these estimates, which are probably pretty close. But he would hold that, since everyone is born Muslim, that the world cannot be at "peace" until all are submissive to Allah. Any method of expansion that succeeds is welcome.

The two basic premises of Christianity, the Trinity and

[1] Mike Konrad, "The Greatest Murder Machine in History", *American Thinker*, May 31, 2014, http://www.americanthinker.com/articles/2014/05/the_greatest_murder_machine_in_history.html.

the Incarnation, are specifically denied in Islamic texts. Indeed, according to Muslim belief, the Bible itself was written after Muhammad's Qur'an with its divine origins. The Bible is a corrupt version of the original. The Qur'an predates Scripture. It predates Adam. Of course, no proof for this remarkable opinion exists. The notion that the Qur'an predates the world was the result of a need to undermine the obvious fact that the Qur'an itself is a later rewriting of Jewish and Christian Scripture. By saying Christ is a "prophet", the Qur'an says implicitly that He is not God.

What Islam and the Bible have in common is very little when it comes to doctrine. As Rémi Brague shows, only with the greatest stretch of the imagination can we say that Muslims believe in the same God as Christians and Jews. What is unique in Islam is that these differences are not really allowed to be discussed in any scientific or objective terms. The fear is obvious, that Islam cannot bear any such analysis.

The accusation of blasphemy against the Qur'an often carries with it a death threat. This threat, implicit or stated, always impedes any real examination of the truth of Islamic positions. In general, those who propose "dialogues" with Islam are forced to talk only of what few things they might have in common or of things said to be of natural human understanding. But a voluntarist philosophy makes any such discussion problematic at best. A divinity that can arbitrarily change its mind leaves no room for human reasoning.

The fact is that no real critical edition of the Qur'an exists, one based on the standards of scientific biblical criticism. There seem to have been many varying texts of the Qur'an in existence before its final redaction decades after Muhammad's death. A group of German scholars has been at work to produce such a critical edition for some time.

But because they feel their lives are threatened, the project requires the greatest circumspection.

In the light of what I have suggested in these reflections, I want to conclude that the great challenge that the Islamic State presents to the world has to be that of the truth or falsity of Islam itself. If the true interpretation of what the Qur'an says of Islam is that of the founders of the Islamic State, as I tend to think that it is, we can no longer avoid careful public examination of the incoherence that is found in Islam itself. We talk of respecting another man's views, but if his views include widespread cultural and personal destruction, as they do in the case of Christians and others in the Islamic State, the examination of these views becomes much more pressing. The centuries-long failure to come to grips with what Islam says of itself must come to a close.

This examination does not obviate the diplomatic and military efforts simply to stop the killing. But that endeavor is just a temporary solution, if it works at all. Until the broader issue is frankly faced, as it really has not been since the inception of Islam's wars of expansion, the problem will always recur. The most important "political" thing we can do is to face a theological position that encourages and justifies a religion in its efforts to submit the world to Allah. The people who seek to do this are, for the most part, sincere and earnest in their views. They think them true. The question is: Are they right? Is this what the world is about on the basis of their explanations of it? The failure to answer this issue is one of the most curious facts in all of intellectual history.

13

Lessons of Paris 1/7

Not to minimize their importance, but atrocities on the scale of the Paris attacks of January 7, 2015, which included the murder of twelve people at the office of satirical magazine *Charlie Hebdo,* have been occurring for years in various places in the world, as Michael Coren (*Hatred: Islam's War on Christianity*) and others have recorded in gory detail. In two weeks or months, we will have other killings staged in a similar dramatic manner for the same given reason—blasphemy for insulting Muhammad or the Qur'an. It matters little where they happen.

But killings in Paris, New York, London, Rome, Munich, Sydney, and Bombay are more attention grabbing than slaughters in the backwaters and deserts of Nigeria, Iraq, Sudan, or the Philippines. The central question, for the moment, is this: Are these murders to be attributed to Islam itself, or are they the "aberrations" of fanatic splinter sects?

Muslim organizations alternate between enthusiastic approval and cautious denial of responsibility for attacks against non-Muslims. Liberals talk of absolute freedoms of speech

Adapted from "Lessons from Paris", *MercatorNet*, January 15, 2015, https://www.mercatornet.com/articles/view/lessons_from_paris.

and religion, not just of Muslims. Ideologues find a nonreligious reason for the violence like poverty, exploitation, or envy. Christians want the killings and second-class citizenship stopped everywhere. To this end, the pope has called for an international conference. Historians examine the validity of Qur'anic claims to have a coherent origin and development. Philosophers cite the voluntarism that Muslim thinkers have taken, a step that justifies the jihadist position. Theologians seem loath to analyze the Qur'an's claim to be a genuine "revelation" that specifically denies basic Christian doctrines. German scholars work on a critical edition of the Qur'an to demonstrate its original sources.

Even the president of Egypt is concerned. At al-Azhar University, President al-Sisi said that the Islamic religion needs to "revolutionize" itself. It is not an "ideology". Muslims cannot hope to kill all the other people on the planet in the name of their religion just so Allah can rule the remainder. Some hold a kind of "two-Islam" theory: a peaceful Islam that denies violent methods though holding on to the rest of Muslim teachings, and a radical Islam that justifies violence in Muslim history and in the Qur'an. The four legal schools of Muslim tradition are brought in. Some want to have Islam "modernize" or "secularize" itself. Others see it as moral force in the world reacting to the decadence of the West. All admit that some justification for jihad is found in the Qur'an and Muslim history. Some say Islam is obsolete; others maintain that the real Islam now finally is regaining its power.

Defining Islam

The question of what the Islamic religion is can no longer be avoided. Even universities may seriously examine this issue and not sidestep it with evasions in the name of diversity or multiculturalism. My own initial reactions to the Paris murders on January 7, 2015, were these:

1. This is the French 9/11.

2. It is not mainly about "free speech".

3. Many such attacks are stopped every day by police and other forces in the United States, Canada, France, and even Russia, China, India, Australia, and other European countries. Such attacks are not all merely "accidentally related". They cannot be attributed to something called "terrorists" with no relation to Islam itself.

4. The question Pope Benedict posed was "whether Allah approved vengeance or killing in the name of religion". This remains the right question. Twelve French citizens were gunned down in the name of Allah. This act was according to the letter of Islamic law. The French president insisted that these attacks had "nothing to do with religion". This view is incoherent. His position was a "noble lie", probably made in his mind to prevent civil war.

5. The main reason many Muslims are in France and other countries is demographic—the lack of indigenous children, the multiplicity of Muslim children. This is another story, but one bound up with the intellectual understanding of our era.

6. Islamic immigrants generally do not assimilate into a new culture but quickly form their own enclaves from which "foreigners", that is, local police and populace, are excluded. Many Muslim thinkers have plotted out this process of how "democratically" to take over a country step-by-step. The new novel *Submission* by Michel Houellebecq describes how it might happen in France itself.

7. Political and economic theories that have embraced large-scale immigration have not understood the religious presuppositions of Muslim immigrants. The attacks on 9/11 and 1/7 require a new political realism that is not totalitarian, nationalist, or naive. It must be one capable of understanding what the young men who killed the twelve Frenchmen and those who praised their bloody deeds were shouting as they killed them. Many Christians have been killed to the same shout during the past months in the Middle East, Africa, and elsewhere. Why have we paid little attention?

8. Not a few Muslims, thank God, abhor such killings. We all would like to see this abhorrence expressed not just in terms of "It was not I" but in terms of effective action by Muslims themselves based on sources in their own law and philosophy, not ours. We know that the effort can be lethal for them also. The question many ask is: Can it be done at all?

The Recovery of Reason

What are we to make of Islam's being recognized, even by many of its own members, as a problem in itself, if not the world problem?

First, we must understand that the Islamic State conceives itself to be the true Islam. Its apologists maintain that they represent the authentic understanding of Islam's scripture and tradition. The Islamic people who disagree with them are both cowards and heretics. They too will be dealt with. The aim of the new caliphate is nothing less than world conquest, so that Islamic law is accepted by all people as Allah's will.

The use of violence to accomplish this end is justified in the Qur'an and in philosophic voluntarism that explains how Allah can at one time talk of peace and next talk of war, without any problem. Reason has no place in this system. The world itself and all events in it are directly caused by Allah's will. There are no secondary causes. This view explains the lack of much serious science in the Islamic world once voluntarism came to rule its mind. If something can always be otherwise, no basis exists to examine anything.

Some Muslims deny that the Islamic State's claims have anything to do with Islam. But how is it possible to explain its expansion and its atrocities as unrelated to Islam? One way maintains that it is all a just reaction to turmoil and war imposed by others on Islam. Another way is to rely on legal interpreters who emphasize milder parts of the Qur'an. It is a matter of interpretation.

What seems to be lacking is a standard, be it of reason or natural law, whereby the text and tradition of violence that are found in Muslim practice can be judged as objectively wrong. As long as the Qur'an is regarded as a divine revelation, someone will always arise to imitate the Islamic State's interpretation of the duties of Muslims to make everyone subject to Allah.

When one comes right down to it, it seems that, on its own grounds, the "legitimate" interpretation of Islam is the interpretation of the victor. If the caliphate manages to take over increasing areas, including direct control of existing Muslim states, parts of Europe, and more, it will be held to be Allah's will and justified on the grounds of success. This rationale justified original Muslim conquests of Byzantine, Persian, Hindu, and African lands.

Christians often do not realize that many lands that were once Christian are now Muslim by conquest with no hope of return. Many unknown and unrecognized Christian martyrs almost daily witness to suffering that does not seem to convert Muslims to Christianity. The Qur'an is said to be mildly sympathetic to people of the Book; it states that Jesus is a prophet, it venerates Mary, and it offers them second-class citizenship rather than death. Islam is eager to convert Christians and is often successful, while a Muslim who becomes a Christian risks his life. These positions are hardly encouraging.

The real intellectual question is the validity of the Islamic claim that the content of Islam's revelation originates in God. But there are many reasons to be skeptical, in addition to the apparent sanctioning of practices that other cultures regard as deeply inhumane, like slavery, mutilation, violent jihad, subordination of women, and so on. There are scriptural reasons too: Islam accepts the "Gospel of Jesus" but rejects key doctrines taught by Jesus, like the Incarnation and the Trinity. The claim that the Qur'an "predates" the Old and New Testaments is preposterous.

Can a religion that contains all these problematic issues claim to be a true revelation? Can a revelation be true if God left no authority to determine authentic interpretation of its scriptures? These fundamental questions have been opened up by the series of atrocities that has culminated in 1/7 in Paris. It is a crisis for Islam, as President al-Sisi implied. But Muslims should not let this crisis go to waste. This is their chance to synchronize reason and faith, their chance to show that being human and being deeply religious are compatible, their chance to repudiate the barbarity of unforgiving men and to let the mercy of their God shine forth.

14

On the Beheading of Christians

Sandro Magister's account of the beheading and subsequent canonization of twenty-one Egyptian Coptic Christians in Libya, with the name of each man killed, was heartbreaking and poignant.[1] I must confess that when I heard the next day the remarks of Benjamin Netanyahu to the U.S. Congress in which he said, defiantly, that Israel is now armed and will defend itself, I felt a touch of envy. Our spiritual and temporal leaders can barely bring themselves to mention the terrible persecution that Christians in too many lands now regularly undergo.

Magister recalled that these Copts had originally fled from Iraq to Egypt, as if to warn us that there is no longer any hiding place. These Christians literally had no one to defend them. No Christian armies exist. The words of Christian leaders are usually "Why does not someone else protect

---

Adapted from "On the Beheading of Christians", *MercatorNet*, March 10, 2015, https://www.mercatornet.com/articles/view/on_the_beheading_of_christians/15762.

[1] Sandro Magister, "Saint Milad Saber and His Twenty Companions", *Chiesa*, March 2, 2015, http://chiesa.espresso.repubblica.it/articolo/1351000?eng=y.

us?" Appealing to the United Nations is like "blowin' in the wind".

Urban II, who convoked the Crusades, somehow, is looking better every time we hear of massive killings of Christians and others by Muslims who claim, with justification in their own minds, that they carry out the will of Allah. To Christians, these acts are terrible atrocities. To Muslims carrying out these deeds, they are acts of war and piety.

What ought to be done with these killers if ever captured? Many people who ask themselves this, even if they favor the abolition of the death penalty, will answer, "Shoot them at dawn." The killers show no sorrow or repentance, only a defiant courage that stops at nothing. If freed, they will continue the killings. Islamic State (ISIS) poses a real dilemma for those who want to abolish capital punishment, especially for Christians.

Of course, if, rather than imprisoning them for a few years after a civil trial lasting three or four years, their captors did shoot them at dawn, much of the Muslim world would be in the streets protesting and look on them as "martyrs". Such is our world.

The "separation of church and state", however wise, has left us with an American president and other world leaders who cannot acknowledge either that it is Christians who are being killed or that it is Muslims who kill them. The killers are said to be just "terrorists", an absolutely meaningless designation. They kill to advance a cause that they believe in, not just to kill. "Terrorism for its own sake" explains no actual group in the Muslim world.

In this case, it was the Muslim leaders of Egypt who behaved honorably, putting to shame their Western counterparts. The prime minister and the impressive president separately visited the families of the Coptic martyrs. They promised aid and help to build a church in their honor. These are good Muslim leaders, even though they were the ones most capable of preventing these particular killings. The Coptic Church, bless it, immediately canonized these young men—no ecclesiastical delay there.

How are we to think of these things? If we are not enraged by them, there is probably something wrong with us. Unlike Augustine's friend Alypius, who finally could not resist gazing at the killings in Roman gladiatorial combats, I cannot bear to watch clips of these beheadings. There is something diabolical about them, even something diabolical about knowing they are going on and doing nothing about them.

Again, what are we to think of these deaths? First of all, in the mind of the killers, it does not matter to which "branch" of Christianity one belongs. Pope Francis talks of an "ecumenism of martyrdom". Indeed, it does not really matter if one is a Christian. The whole culture that is not Muslim is said to be guilty and a legitimate object of war.

What about the thousands and thousands of Christians who have been killed? Christian peoples and even buildings are being eliminated from within the Muslim world. Will there be any place to which to flee? Are we all to suffer the fate of the Iraqi Copts who fled to Egypt, only to be slaughtered there a few decades later? What seems clear is that we have no leadership willing and able to understand the theological roots and consequent practices that justify these killings.

What is left?

Two of the Coptic men who were killed were brothers. A third brother, Beshir Kamel, was asked what he would do if he saw a member of the Islamic State who murdered his brothers. Kamel replied that the ISIS tapes of the beheading of his brothers and their companions did not edit out their final profession of faith in Christ before they were decapitated. We know they died martyrs, he said. He then referred to his mother and what she would do: "My mother, an uneducated woman in her sixties, says she would ask [the killer] to enter her house and ask God to open his eyes because he was the reason her sons entered the kingdom of heaven."[2]

The immediate response to the beheadings is up in the air. Some think we should pull out and let the Arabs fight it out among themselves. Others want American intervention to knock out ISIS. Perhaps Islam will reform itself? Or Turkey will take over the area? Israel might strike, or be wiped out. ISIS may succeed in overturning the Saudi monarchy or regain Egypt.

Yet, whatever the immediate policies or fates, surely we have here the ultimate answer, spoken by an uneducated Coptic woman.

Militant Islam, if it is doing nothing else, is busy populating the Kingdom of God. Meanwhile, an increasingly relativist culture doubts that there is any transcendent purpose in individual human lives. Hence, it averts its eyes in such a way that the beheadings are hardly noticed except as added dramas on the evening news. They are hardly distinguishable from the fictional violence that is shown on television every day. The fine line between reality and image is confused. Actual events like the beheading of twenty-one Egyptian Copts are merely added incidents in a busy day of imagining how we can improve the world. "Coptic martyrs of Libya, pray for us."

---

[2] "Coptic Church Recognizes Martyrdom of 21 Coptic Christians", News.va, http://www.news.va/en/news/coptic-church-recognizes-martyrdom-of-21-coptic-ch.

15

Dialogues without Resolutions

In recent decades, the Church has sponsored responsible dialogues with almost every religion and philosophical position. These dialogues are not debates from which we expect a winner and a loser. Their burden is rather clarity. If knowledgeable Baptists or Buddhists agree to enter formal discussions with the Catholic Church about what each has in common and in what they differ, the purpose is not "evangelization", as Catholics call it, nor is it proselytism. Rather it is to clear away misunderstandings about what one or the other party might hold to be true, together with an explanation of the grounds on which one's view is held to be valid. The assumption is that, while, in principle, fundamental disagreements may exist, the problems that are based on confusions of terminology, misunderstandings of meaning, or historical conditions alone ought not to be left unresolved.

The spirit of such dialogue is fraternal. The parties are willing to set aside hostility and, yes, arms. Where agreement is possible, it should be admitted. Where it is not, the

First published as the preface to *The Caliph al-Mahdi and the Patriarch Timothy I: An 8th Century Interreligious Dialogue*, by Wafik Nasry (CreateSpace Independent Publishing Platform, 2015).

terms of disagreement should be stated accurately by everyone involved. Often, such dialogue has to take place in private. Passions, prejudices, or publicity can easily interfere with genuine efforts accurately to set forth differences. It is assumed, moreover, that men want to have these differences made known and, if possible, resolved. We must grant that this openness is not always the case. Genuine dialogue sometimes needs protection from outside moral and physical threats. This issue has long been hammered out over the nature of academic and religious freedom. The Catholic Church, in fact, holds that religious freedom is the most basic freedom on which all others depend. The freedom to know and worship God truthfully can be the only real foundation of human dignity.

This considered approach to dialogue has been especially true of Muslim-Christian relations. Muslims and Christians have, in fact, been locked in dialogue of one form or another almost since Islam first appeared on the scene out of Arabia in the seventh century. It became especially significant in the following centuries when Islamic armies conquered lands of Syrian, Byzantine, Persian, and Coptic Christians. The process whereby the conquerors gradually, but steadily, converted conquered residents of the new Islamic lands is well known. Much of the early scholarship on Islam was done by Christians or ex-Christians. Except for later reconquests in Spain and southern Europe, lands still claimed to be Muslim by right of conquest and conversion, the Muslim religion and its political expression remain dominant if not exclusive. Practically, the Islamic world extends from Morocco across the world to Indonesia and North India. Few conversions of Islamic peoples to Christianity or to anything else have taken place over the centuries. The reasons for this stability are in part explained by the internal moral and physical force used within Islam to prevent any slippage from the faith.

In the nineteenth and twentieth centuries, many of the Muslim countries were administered by European powers —England, France, Italy, Holland, and Spain. The Western model of public rule with parliaments, courts, and elections still is in place on the surface, at least. Since the fall of Marxism and the decline of European birthrates, however, Islam is no longer confined to its classical borders; it has established a significant and growing presence throughout Europe and the United States as well as southern Africa. In the light of a clear decline in Christian vitality, Islam has often taken its place as the most dynamic and aggressive religious movement. Basic Islamic theory holds that the whole world should worship Allah and live according to Islamic law. The mission of Islam is to make this happen. In recent years, many Muslim thinkers have rejected the modernization approach to Islamic problems with the modern world to advocate instead a return to strict observance of the Sharia within Islamic countries as the will of Allah. The notion of "holy war" is often designed to achieve this universal purpose.

This book (*The Caliph al-Mahdi and the Patriarch Timothy I: An 8th Century Interreligious Dialogue* by Wafik Nasry) records the dialogue between the third Abbasid caliph, al-Mahdi, and Timothy, the first Nestorian patriarch in 781. The two men met in Baghdad, a city which, at the time, had become the seat of Muslim power. It had recently been transferred from Damascus. Indeed, Muslim Baghdad of this and later eras became, among many thinkers, a symbol of the real alternative to Athens, Jerusalem, or Rome. While Athens looked to the philosophers, Jerusalem to revelation, and Rome to their mutual coherence, Baghdad came from the Averroist position of the primacy of the philosophers within Islam. The famous "double truth" theory, which arose over the question of reason and revelation, had its cultural defenders. Reason and revelation could contradict each other. That is, both parts of a contradiction could be true. The public order was to be left to "faith" to "religion" to Islam, for the control of the masses of people in the society for whom blind faith was all that mattered.

In the meantime, the philosophers would live quiet lives of relative peace and luxury in Baghdad or some other elegant and genteel city. They would carry on their philosophic reflections in freedom without fear of the fate of Socrates or Christ. But their private lives and discussions would be outside public attention. On the surface, the philosopher would appear in the garb and guise of the official religion. He would attend the rites, but he would not necessarily hold any of its propositions except as myths. Other cities might accept or reject revelation, but Baghdad would be the city where the best regime existed, the best that could be expected. Islam was not really "true" but it controlled the public order by custom and force. The true philosopher showed his superiority over the contradictory myths of Islam by his quiet life of reflection.

But the conversation of al-Mahdi and Timothy is not of this character, except that it does take place in quiet. It also takes place before the philosophy of al-Ghazali (d. 1111) came to dominate Muslim thought.[1] This was a philosophy based on the primacy of will (voluntarism). Pope Benedict, in his Regensburg lecture, touched on this issue in referring to a later dialogue between a Persian gentleman and Byzan-

---

[1] See Robert Reilly, *The Closing of the Muslim Mind* (Wilmington: ISI Books, 2011).

tine Emperor Manuel II Paleologus (1391).[2] That dialogue was concerned with the issue of whether Islam caused more evil than good, whether it approved expansion by violence according to its religious tenets and historical record. Voluntarism was a will theory that enabled one to say, and enabled Allah to advise, that violence was both right and wrong, that Allah could, as texts in the Qur'an showed, change his mind to make what was good evil or evil good. What counted was the will of Allah, not his consistency. Consistency is not an issue in a voluntarist system.

This will-change possibility implied that what was true or good could also become false or bad if Allah so willed. His power, it was held, would be lessened if he could not make evil good or good evil. This view supposedly resolved the contradictions that appeared in the text of the Qur'an where violence was both advocated and not advocated.[3] Moreover, the logic of voluntarism meant that no objective order existed against which to test actions. Things could always be otherwise. Hence, no problem existed between reason and revelation. There was no order in nature. Anything could be its opposite. This view also makes science impossible as it depends on stable secondary causes. In his lecture, the pope touched on the similarity of this voluntarist view in Islam to views in modern Western philosophy.

The dialogue between Caliph al-Mahdi and Patriarch Timothy I has a long history in its preservation and translation into modern languages. The book gives this background.

[2] See James V. Schall, *The Regensburg Lecture* (South Bend: St. Augustine's, 2007).

[3] See Samir Khalil Samir, *111 Questions on Islam: Samir Khalil Samir, S.J., on Islam and the West*, a series of interviews conducted by Giorgio Paolucci and Camille Eid, trans. and ed. by Wafik Nasry (San Francisco: Ignatius Press, 2008).

In addition, we have several versions of the conversation, though they seem to be in basic harmony. The editors, Wafik Nasry and Samir Khalil Samir, have done considerable research on this document. It serves to emphasize the importance of the famous conversation. We do not have a text from the caliph, but a letter from Timothy recounting the conversation.

The caliph bases his questions on the Qur'an and Muslim tradition, though he has read at least some of the Old and New Testaments. No philosophers are mentioned by either party. Though Timothy is a Nestorian bishop, all of his answers about the two natures and one person in Christ follow the early councils of the Church that dealt with these questions. Nestorians were said to hold that Mary could not be called the Mother of God. Timothy admits that Christ's human nature involved but one divine Person, not two different persons or beings. As Muslim thought also denied that Christ was the Son of God, but only a prophet, it is striking that Timothy here defends the unity of the two natures, separate but real in the one divine Person of Christ.

In a first reading, the text will seem odd in the way issues are resolved. For example, we might expect that the fact of Mohammed coming some six hundred years after Christ would scientifically be enough to settle the issue of which religion came first. But within Islam an elaborate defensive view was developed. It maintains that no mention of Mohammed is found in Christian texts because, at some point, about which no evidence exists, all Jewish and Christian manuscripts were purged of these references. The only trouble with this theory, besides its intrinsic implausibility, is, as Timothy pointed out to the caliph, that no evidence of such a purging exists.

Moreover, it seems that Judaism is obviously older than either Islam or Christianity. Yet, another Muslim theory holds that the Qur'an existed in Allah or heaven before Creation. It was set forth in its original form as a message to Mohammed. This entails the theory that everyone was originally Muslim but lost his faith through influence of parents or other sources. Muslims thus maintain that everyone is Muslim originally but has unjustly lost his faith. Hence bringing everyone back to Islam is the mission of Islam so that all worship Allah in the only way allowed, that found in the Qur'an.

The issue of the scientific status of the Qur'anic text or texts will not, of course, come up in this conversation. The use of form criticism and other research tools on the Qur'an itself is a project undertaken by German scholars in Berlin and its results will certainly help illuminate the kind of conversation that appears here. But what is striking, as one reads this text, is the effort of both Muslim and Christian to show the reasonability of his position. As the authors note, very often Muslims do not know Christian or Jewish texts but only those references to Christ or the prophets found in the Qur'an.

A good deal of the conversation in this text concerns simply the right understanding of what Christians hold about the Trinity and the Incarnation. As both of these doctrines are specifically denied in the Qur'an, Timothy has to show how they make sense. When asked why he is not a follower of Mohammed, Timothy explains that nothing about Mohammed is found in either the Old or New Testaments. He gives this sort of answer both because the Muslim holds the text of the Qur'an to contain all that is necessary to know and that it does in certain texts "implicitly" refer to

Mohammed while not mentioning his name. The task of Timothy then becomes simply one of showing that these texts do not refer to Mohammed.

Issues such as the virginity of Mary after the birth of Christ are handled by analogy. The question of the Trinity and the unity of God is central for the Muslim. How is it that Christians hold that there are three gods? Or how is it that if Christ died, He was not truly God? Timothy responds with a basic treatise in Christology but in terms that would be acceptable to the Muslim, at least in theory. Christians do not believe in three gods. They hold that Christ was both God and man but one Person and that divine.

The structure of this text recorded by Timothy is such that we read through its essential parts twice. This is accomplished by translating different versions of the text. It is quite useful for those who are reading this way of argument for the first time. The caliph poses precise questions. The patriarch answers them. The two do not argue much. They seem content to know what the other presents. No question of conversion or change of mind ever comes up.

When we come to the end of the text, we realize that the caliph and the patriarch have not changed any of their basic positions. The caliph seems satisfied that the responses are respectful to Muslim positions, even though they disagree with the wording of the text in the Qur'an. The Muslim view is that a further revelation, after that of the prophets and Christ, took place with Mohammed. The last revelation, which was the handing down of the text of the Qur'an in Arabic from its eternal place, takes precedence over the others. What is last is always the authentic text. Hence anything that is found in the Qur'an that contradicts what is in the Old or New Testament must be right.

Timothy has to take the position that nothing in the Old

or New Testaments predicted or prophesied the coming of Mohammed.[4] In fact, the revelation in Christ was the last and definitive one. From the Christian view, the Qur'an has no authority and is not of divine origin, particularly because it denies the truth of the basic Christian positions.

But it can be said, I think, that this early dialogue does fulfill the purpose of the later ones of our time in the sense that it does clarify just how an intelligent Muslim leader thinks about what he knows of Christianity. It does give the response to these concerns of the Muslim in terms that arise from sources he would respect or understand. Most of the same issues that separate Muslims and Christians are still in effect. It is proof that clarity is not the whole answer to the relations and truth of these religions.

What we do have here are "dialogues without resolution". This result does not mean that truth is not to be found. It is not a skeptical conclusion. We must remember that Timothy was present before the caliph as the latter's political subject. He had been befriended and even was exempt from the tax that Muslims forced Jews and Christians to pay for civil tolerance. Thus, there was not really that freedom present that might lead to a conclusion that some part of these positions is simply wrong and must be rejected. Argument did not change the caliph's culture.

With a voluntarist background, we are brought back to the Regensburg lecture and whether religion can be spread by violence. Timothy did not bring up to the caliph the issue of the rapid spread of Islam through conquest. But the caliph did bring up the issue of the Cross, which he took to be a sign of weakness and proof that Christ could not have

<hr />

[4] See Rémi Brague, *On the God of the Christians (and on One or Two Others)* (South Bend, Ind.: St. Augustine's, 2013).

been God. Gods do not die. Again Timothy explained the difference between Christ's human and divine nature.

The caliph also wanted to show that, if Christ willingly suffered for our sins, then the Jews were not guilty. Timothy distinguishes, that is, he uses a philosophy that accepts the principle of contradiction and is not voluntarist. Neither the Jew nor the Muslim recognizes Christ as the Son of God. Christ did lay down His life for our sins voluntarily. But this fact did not mean that the Jews and the Romans who executed Him were simply guiltless. They unjustly executed an innocent man. They failed to recognize that by doing so they fulfilled Scripture. In making Christ to be a mere prophet, the Muslims too reject Him as the Son of God who was one with His Father.

This text of a dialogue from the eighth century, in conclusion, brings back to life what at first sight appears a very formal and rather elevated dialogue between a caliph and a patriarch. When we read it, however, we find ourselves again involved with ancient controversies that remain with us every day. This text is an invitation for us again to think through basic theological and philosophical questions that simply will not go away until they are resolved in truth.

16

On the "Causes of Terrorism"

The killing of four Marines and a sailor at a recruiting station in Chattanooga, Tennessee (July 16, 2015), by a lone, unattached gunman—but one with clear Muslim cultural and ideological connections—again brings up the question, perplexing to so many, about the why of such lethal actions.

Attacks of this kind are not in fact all that unusual, either in the United States or elsewhere. Neither are they purposeless. Indeed, they indicate a well-thought-out systematic approach whereby a Muslim army, with a base in the Near East, can mastermind such attacks anywhere in the world with the help of normal technology and young men willing to give up their lives in the cause.

I want to approach this question of "terrorism" initially by way of a remark I heard on Fox News in discussing the Tennessee shootings. A commentator stated, quite bluntly, "If Muhammad were to return to the world today to indicate which Muslim group was best representing his authentic heritage and teaching, he would vigorously affirm that it was ISIS and al-Qaida."

Adapted from "What Causes This Terrorist Scourge?", *MercatorNet*, July 27, 2015, https://www.mercatornet.com/articles/view/what-causes-this-terrorist-scourge/16566.

This is, of course, the one view that cannot be mentioned in polite discourse even in Islam itself. Indeed, it is against the law in many countries, not just Muslim ones, to thus criticize Islam. It violates the liberal and ecumenical minds in their theoretic views about equality and respect. But the nagging question remains: Is this statement true?

Let me approach this issue in a roundabout way. An article in the July 3, 2015, edition of *L'Osservatore Romano* concerns the Holy See's "Statement to the United Nations". The headline reads: "The Answer to Terrorism Cannot Be a Military Response". The same page silhouettes three black-clad ISIS men. They stand defiantly against the sky with tommy guns raised on high. One wonders what these three men would think of this "no military response" view. No doubt they would be quite amused. They would interpret it as another example of the effeteness of their opponents.

Like most military men, ISIS fighters understand that their base of operation on the ground is the immediate, but not ultimate, foundation of their ability to carry out their mission in the wider world. Air strikes will not stop their effectiveness. They have found a way to bypass armies by striking at the civilians who support them. If one reads Archbishop Silvano Tomasi's text carefully, however, he did not exactly say what the headline says. He was more nuanced: "The response to terrorism cannot be *merely* by way of military action." The notion that we can deal with ISIS without effective military action at some level is simply naive, utopian, or both.

Archbishop Tomasi, the permanent observer of the Holy See to the United Nations, had given an address to the Human Rights Council in Geneva. The full-page text follows the above-cited headline. The photo of the ISIS fighters stand in the middle of the text. The archbishop noted the "terrorist" attacks in the Middle East and different parts of Africa. Since 2000, a "staggering" five hundred percent increase in such destruction has occurred. The only mention of the names of the attackers was in his statement referring to the "innocent victims at the hands of ISIS and Boko Haram groups". Over 80 percent of the killings were in five states: Iraq, Afghanistan, Pakistan, Nigeria, and Syria. But we need to concern ourselves with the "negative effects of terrorism on the enjoyment of our rights and fundamental freedoms". The fact that almost all the terrorism cited by the archbishop is Islamic was delicately not mentioned. Instead, something called "terrorism" is the cause of terrorism.

Terrorism Cannot Cause Itself

What then are the causes of terrorism? These causes are what we need to know, not just the effects. If these causes are not squarely addressed, both the states involved and the international community will suffer. The Holy See is especially concerned by attacks on religion. Whether some religion can be a cause of terrorism is not mentioned, though it is implied that it cannot be. Next follows in the text a definition: "Terrorism is a political means to influence behavior and to reach objectives through fear."

But this definition does not tell us why anyone would want to use these means. It tells us terrorism's effects, not its cause. Terrorism cannot cause itself. It is not something for its own sake, as if no end of terrorism is envisioned by those who carry it out. What they envision in fact is peace, the "peace of Islam". The only way we can know these objectives is to ask those who use terror. We cannot just say that the cause of "terrorism" is "terrorism".

Terrorism has become globalized. "Terrorism is the antithesis of the shared values and commitments which serve as the basis for peaceful coexistence domestically and internationally", the text reads.

This view assumes that ISIS and al-Qaida leaders think that what they see in the West is a peaceful, contented life. Rather, what they see are drugs, violence, prejudice, abortion, perversion, infidelity, and the whole range of moral disorders that our governments seek to tolerate or impose on others.

The ISIS members do not see themselves as "terrorists". They are just avengers of Allah. It is ideological blindness not to see a well-thought-out, voluntarist-based, and religious origin behind the actual terrorism that we confront.

Tomasi notes that the terrorists are often supported by certain governments in supplying arms and other necessities. He does not speculate on why supposedly peaceful Muslims might quietly support ISIS. He does not mention the enormous number of mosques built in Europe and America. The archbishop notes that "the greatest violation is complete contempt for innocent human life, the basic right on which all other human rights are founded." It needs to be stated here, however, that the term "innocent human life" is one that grows out of Western thought.

The Muslim fighter does not see the non-Muslim as innocent, which is why agreement on even this issue is almost impossible. The man who shot the Marines expected to reach heaven because of his deed. Being killed while killing an infidel is often conceived as itself a martyrdom. "Terrorism does not respect the dignity of its victims." This is because the idea of dignity is a foreign idea to Islam. Again, what exactly is this "terrorism"? If all those outside the "peace of

Islam" are considered to be guilty and objects of war, the cause is not some abstraction called "terrorism".

Tomasi turns to the refugees that this terrorism creates. We have a "humanitarian" crisis. There is the destruction of cultural objects, churches, buildings, and art. Again, the theological reason for this destruction explains its rationale. It is not just wanton, random destruction but destruction of specific objects held to be idols or unworthy of Allah. To maintain that the Muslim should not destroy the idols in alien cultures is asking him to violate his religious beliefs. Dialogue about humanitarianism will not prevent this destruction. Humanism is not the basis of the Muslim's thinking about these things seen as blasphemous.

"By destroying the infrastructure of cities and regions, especially by attacking government buildings, schools and religious institutions, terrorism literally brings a society to its knees." This statement, while true, assumes that terrorism is undertaken for its own sake. The reason why a society is brought to its knees is that it might be replaced by the caliphate, by Muslim rule and faith. We are often shocked by "the annihilation of history of cultures and civilizations". Yet, it is not shocking if one thinks that these things are themselves signs of alien gods and ought not to exist in the first place.

"It can hardly be doubted that terrorism has political effects and influences the political process, at least in a democratic and particularly in a democratic state." Archbishop Tomasi warns of counterterrorism efforts that themselves violate rights. Such efforts can cause a countertyranny. This point is valid but often also prevents Western governments from stopping groups like ISIS from causing chaos in their cities.

"The most obvious way in which terrorism can influence the political process is by bringing about changes in public opinion. . . . It can be very hard for Governments to resist the pressure from public opinion for a strong reaction in the wake of a terrorist attack." We do not have any "uniform" response to terrorist attacks. The Holy See agrees that terrorism needs to be confronted at all levels, not just militarily.

The Ultimate Cause of Contemporary Global Terrorism

When the cause of the violence and turmoil is named "terrorism", it leaves us with a vague, amorphous something that has no organized membership, geography, or purpose. The common approach to terrorism is in line with that depicted by Archbishop Tomasi. But is it possible to conceive another way to think about these issues?

The first step, it strikes me, is to face the fact that ISIS and other movements are, as they claim to be, directly related to the Qur'an, its interpretation, and the expansionist history of earlier Muslim armies that conquered northern Africa, the Near East, and many of the lands to the east of Persia. ISIS is not making up out of the clouds its understanding of the teaching of the Qur'an. It is carrying on, and claims to be carrying on, a tradition and enterprise that has been present for some twelve centuries. The most surprising thing about this fact is to be surprised by it.

The proof of Islam, moreover, is the success of Islam in ever expanding itself. The Islam we see today is energized, not hindered, by the successes of the violent endeavors, beginning with 9/11 and the worldwide Muslim reaction to it. This same idea is behind the present realization of Islam that it can, by these violent means, make enormous gains in places that once defeated Muslim armies, such as in France and in Vienna.

They do not need sophisticated land armies. Among those migrating to the West are numerous men and women bent on changing the nations of Europe and America from within, either by population growth and election, or by force and terror. No "peaceful" Muslim body or nation will oppose this success in any real sense. This is why we cannot simply talk of the "immigrant crisis" as if it has nothing to do with Muslim ambitions to expand. It is also an invasion problem.

We must stop thinking of the terrorists as "terrorists". They are self-confessed followers of Islam as it is set down in its books and as it has consistently manifested itself in history. We have to stop insisting that violence in the name of Allah has nothing to do with Islam but is due simply to a group of "fundamentalists" who are fanatics and can make no coherent case for themselves within Muslim scholarship itself.

Whatever they are, they are clear-eyed thinkers, both as to the nature and the weakness of their immediate enemy and about the *spiritual* goal they seek, nothing less than the world in submission to Allah. This is what their jihad is all about. I see nothing wrong with giving the Muslim leaders who follow this path credit for following their religious purpose, something we cannot admit as possible because of our theories about dialogue, religion, and human nature. These ISIS-type leaders should not be dismissed as mad, insane, fanatic, or fundamentalist but should be seen as men logically carrying out their religious beliefs as found in their sources.

The Catholic Church and Militant Islam

The Catholic Church—and Christianity in general—has never really faced the implications of what the Qur'an says of her. A direct and open denial of the truth of Christianity is found. It does not hesitate to state its critique of Christianity as a false understanding of God. Part of the reluctance to evaluate the truth of Islam is that any criticism of Islam could be and often is lethal. The number of Christian martyrs in Islam grows exponentially today.[1] If someone is killed because a Muslim thought it blasphemous to criticize Islam's tenets, the blame rests not on the Muslim but on the one who criticized.

Yet, it seems strange that the Church has not been more forthright in confronting what the Qur'an says of Christianity itself. In a way, the Church has taken no official notice of Islam's teachings about her. The Crusades were a not-wholly-successful effort, after much provocation and loss, to save what was left of the West. Though there was Saint John Damascene and Aquinas' *Summa contra gentiles*, we have no brief, succinct authoritative statement about the truth of specific Muslim claims about Christian belief itself.

What Islam holds about Christianity's own beliefs is no secret. We are told what Islam holds Christianity to be. If its analysis is right, there is no reason to be a Christian. So it seems, sooner or later, these beliefs must be stated and one by one rejected.

Christians have often clearly formulated positions affirmed against them. The Church has affirmed her own positions about herself. Much of what Islam rejects about Chris-

---

[1] See George Marlin, *Christian Persecutions in the Middle East: A 21st Century Tragedy* (South Bend, Ind.: St. Augustine's, 2015); Michael Coren, *Hatred: Islam's War on Christianity* (Toronto, Ont.: McClelland and Stewart, 2014).

tianity—that Christians believe there are "three gods", for instance—are simply errors. It requires much reasoning to establish and clarify how there can be one God but three Persons.

Let us look at some basic Muslim views on the truth of which the strength of the ISIS arms depends. ISIS would not be fighting if it thought these positions were not valid.

1. The original divine revelation was the Qur'an directly from Allah. The Old and New Testaments are later corruptions distorting the original text. Therefore, neither are the will of Allah.

2. Originally everyone was born Muslim. Baptism is not necessary. If someone is not Muslim, it is because he has been corrupted by his parents or society.

3. Allah is one. The Trinity, a belief in three gods, is false.

4. Christ was not divine, nor was He crucified. He was but a prophet. He is not the Son of God.

5. Mary is not the Mother of God, but she is a nice lady.

6. The world is divided into two parts, the world of peace and the world of war. The world of peace is Islam, which is at odds with all other nations, who are guilty for not accepting Allah. Therefore, war against them is always just.

7. The mission of Islam is to subject all the world to Allah. World history is carrying out this purpose. This endeavor can sometimes be accomplished without war (e.g., as in Indonesia), but war is usually a necessary means.

8. A holy war against those who are not Muslim is always justified, though sometimes it may be prudent not to pursue it.

9. If Christians or Jews are found within Islam, they must convert, die, or pay a tax for tolerance. They can never be full citizens.

10. The Sharia should be the civil law in every nation.

11. There is no separation between church and state. The state exists to serve the religion.

12. Allah is not ruled by reason (*logos*). His absolute will can be known only in the Qur'an.

13. The Qur'an justifies war and violence in achieving the peace of Islam.

14. Readings in the Qur'an that contradict each other simply mean that Allah is not bound by his own decrees or any distinction between right and wrong.

15. Allah can will one day, say, peace, and violence the next. The latest entries in the Qur'an are the normative ones.

16. Salvation is given to those who submit to Allah, to whatever he wills.

Christianity needs to make it clear that these doctrines, customs, or understandings are untenable both in reason and as revelation. It is not enough to talk of "respect" for another religion when the other religion both denies the very possibility of your beliefs and persecutes you for holding them.

Confronting Islam

The first step needed, then, is the affirmation, from the Christian side, that these views are as such false. They cannot be divine revelations. Many of them contradict reason. Both Muslim and Christian benefit from knowing exactly what the other holds. Most of the confusion related to using the word "terrorism" is due to a hesitation to examine carefully what Islam holds about violence and about Christianity. The Muslim too needs to be constrained to know exactly what Christianity says of itself, not these fanciful doctrines about no divine Christ or no Trinity of Persons as found in the Qur'an. If these views are false, then the Muslim, by assuming the truth of his revelation, is justified in rejecting those who hold them.

The next step is the recognition that ISIS and other what we insist on calling "terrorist" organizations are not wrong to maintain that they find justification for their violent view in the Qur'an itself. They are not making it up. Sufficient justifications are there in the text. Almost all Muslim scholars know this. Some Muslims who have relocated in the West, and even the Egyptian president, talk of "reforming" Islam, of the absurdity of one billion Muslims eliminating six billion unbelievers.

They are in a dilemma, however. As long as these teachings are in fact found in the Qur'an, which is revealed as such directly by Allah, there will always be found readers in Islam who will take it for what it says. They will accuse other Muslims of disloyalty to Muhammad.

This is why, since Islam was founded in the seventh century, we witness wave after wave of holy war. It shows a religious zeal bent on fulfilling the will of Allah. Thus, I think it intellectually wrong to call ISIS-type movements "terrorists" and not what they profess to be, followers of the example of Muhammad and of the teachings legitimately found in the Qur'an.

The only way to confront this recurring phenomenon of continuing expansion throughout history is not with some "reformation within Islam" but with something closer to "conversion" by an intelligent rejection of its teachings about God, Christ, and world conquest. Military defeats of Muslim armies at Tours, Vienna, and other places, even up to today, have put a temporary stop to this expansion. But the cry always rises again from the text and the men who believe it with their lives. Even Western youth increasingly listen to this call.

But is conversion to Christianity possible, or even desirable? The cost of conversion to Christianity is usually too high. Social ostracism and sometimes death follow conversion. In many Muslim areas any conversion effort is simply against the law or custom. The cause of terrorism, in short, is belief in what the Qur'an says is true and mandatory.

The Qur'an says many nice things, to be sure, worthy things. But it does justify this mission to subject the world to Allah. To call ISIS and other groups "fundamentalists" or "terrorists" implies that they are not interpreting their own revelation for what it stands for.

Is a Reformed Islam Possible?

The effort to transform Islam into modern liberal skepticism is laughed at. Looking back at Muhammad's own record of violent, successful conquest, I suspect that if Muhammad were to return, the man on television would be right: Muhammad would be pleased with ISIS and the present-day expansion of Islam in the West and in Russia. The least we can do in honor is to stop denigrating this purpose as if it has to be something else but what it says it is.

And what about the rejecting of this jihadist view altogether? Although there are bloody struggles within Islam between Sunni and Shiite sects for leadership, Islam seems singularly immune to any conversion, either to Christianity or to the modern world ethos.

Can we expect, as it were, a John Paul II effect, which saw a seemingly unbreakable communism suddenly collapse because its ideas were finally recognized as incoherent and evil? Islam has lasted far longer than communism. Certain ideas found in Plato are older than either. Islam's main rival today is probably not what remains of the West but a much longer-lasting China.

There are, it strikes me, two paths open to reorient Islam. Neither is violent. Both are, in some sense, already in use.

The first concerns the critical edition of the Qur'an that has been under way for too long in Berlin. Several Muslim attempts to close it down have been made. The purpose of this project is to apply methods of textual analysis and integrity to the most ancient texts of the Qur'an. Researchers want to ascertain whether the Qur'an could be, in any sense, what it claims to be. It asserts itself to be a direct transfer of the words of Allah through Muhammad in pure Arabic without any intermediaries. As most of the texts before the final redaction of the Qur'an were deliberately destroyed in the hundred or so years after Muhammad, piecing together the origins of the present text is more difficult, but not impossible.

If the text is not what it claims to be, the whole ethos of the Qur'an is undermined.

A second approach, associated with Fathers Zakaria Botros and Samir Khalil Samir, S.J., has to do with the inner integrity of the text of the Qur'an itself. What is its relation to the Old and New Testaments as well as to reason and logic?

When this exercise is calmly presented in Arabic, when ordinary Muslims can listen to it, it creates the lasting impression that the Qur'an is not really what it claims to be. The efforts made to suppress or obstruct these two approaches testify to their potential effectiveness. This approach requires no guns, only patience and thorough knowledge of Arabic and the Islamic tradition. It testifies on both the Muslim and the Christian sides to the possibility of a truth that everyone can accept.

In retrospect, the causes and alternatives to terrorism are ultimately spiritual and intellectual. Pope Benedict proposed a tactical approach based on prudence and caution: no public theological talks, for few are capable of listening.

But at some point, the issue of the truth that ISIS followers claim must be met on solid grounds. The real "causes of terrorism" make us wonder whether ISIS itself is not the best teacher of the direction we must go. They are not fighting just to be fighting. They are fighting for what they believe to be true. If they cannot be met at this level, they deserve to win.

17

An "Act of War": Paris

We continue to ruminate on the French president's description of the killings in Paris on November 13, 2015, as an "act of war". This "act" was not declared ahead of time according to the rules of war.

The French president deals with a movement that does not follow international law. It follows its own rules. Nor is ISIS yet a formally recognized civil state. It has power to make war outside its borders, which are themselves held by right of conquest. Until defeated, it is a de facto state that has to be reckoned with. The country against which this war was launched was France. Everyone knows that the reach of ISIS extends into Germany, England, Belgium, Italy, Spain, Scandinavia, Australia, and the United States. Whether it can penetrate Russia or China remains to be seen, though Russia is clearly concerned about its own Muslim population.

We recall further 9/11, the bombing of a hotel in India, a resort in Bali, and the wars and slaughters in Africa. We also know that Sunni and Shiite Muslims fight each other

Adapted from "An 'Act of War' ", *MercatorNet*, November 17, 2015, https://www.mercatornet.com/articles/view/an-act-of-war/17195.

in the Middle East. Shootings similar to those in Paris have not taken place in Saudi Arabia or in Iran, though the "spirit of ISIS", as the only genuine Islam, haunts every Muslim government bureaucracy.

Turkey and Egypt have the largest military forces near ISIS; surely enough, if they wanted to, to destroy it along with al-Qaida and other related organizations. But, except in rare cases, they do not move. Over a million men under arms are found in the Muslim states in the Near East with equipment often supplied by or purchased from the United States, France, Russia, or elsewhere. Still, they do not act on any significant scale. This noninvolvement tells us much that we need to know about the Muslim world. Muslim governments prefer to step aside to let someone else do it. They cannot evidently afford to be seen as hostile to Islam itself.

The American president [Obama] initially called the Paris killings an attack on "humanity", an abstraction that allowed him not to name the problem. "Humanity" is an abstraction. It bears no arms, makes no declarations of war. It is much easier to fight than real men with real weapons. Abstractions like "terrorists" are all the president can bring himself to mention.

The terrorists do not call themselves "terrorists". Not accurately naming the problem enables one not to do too much about it. Indeed, no such thing as a "terrorist" organization exists except in the ideological minds of the West. ISIS is engaged in Islamic jihad, nothing more, nothing less. What we insist on calling "terror" they call war.

Pope Francis, who had urged all parishes in Europe to take a refugee family, sees Muslim violence as a "piecemeal World War III". This may be right, as we survey the whole scope of turmoil caused by Muslim-related arms over the past thirty years. Yet it is not World War III but a continuation and a revival of a thirteen-hundred-year war against the rest of the world.

Few will believe that such historic memory exists and that such action can keep recurring. But again, who are the participants in this jihadist World War III? Islam versus everyone else, including "peaceful" Muslims? Is this what the pope meant?

The Egyptian president has warned his fellow religionists against thinking that one billion of them could kill six billion others. Historically, in the seventh century, Muhammad's armies began with nothing and conquered a good part of the world in the following two hundred years, ground they still mostly hold. They see themselves as seeking to expand.

ISIS military convoys of cars and trucks seem militarily laughable. Yet they are in power, even when the American president tells us they are "contained". ISIS cells and sympathizers are in many world centers.

Where do these fighters come from? Who supplies their arms, support, and, more importantly, inspiration? Some of the French killers or their supporters have French, German, Syrian, and other passports that get them into places they want to attack. If this attack is the beginning of World War III, who are the enemies? Who are the defenders? Or is everyone guilty? Is it caused by global warming? By poverty? By maldistribution of goods? Or by none of the above? Is it a war of civilization—indeed, a war of a particular religion seeking to complete its assigned mission among men, including recalcitrant Muslims? If it is this all-out war, why cannot we admit it?

Who are the "peaceful" Muslims? Why do we not hear much from them? The American president thinks 99 percent of Muslims are "peaceful". Robert Cardinal Sarah, speaking of his own country, Guinea, wrote: "The religions have always lived peacefully with one another. The Muslims are a majority but they respect each other."[1] This calm relation cannot be said to exist in Nigeria, Sudan, Libya, Somalia, or most places in the Near East. Historically settled relations within Muslim states are subject to rapid change when they come under ISIS-type influence.

With whom do the peaceful Muslims sympathize, the Parisians slaughtered or their killers? It is difficult to tell. They seem more concerned with "retaliation" against themselves than with containing or finding the attackers. Some Muslim clerics and leaders do condemn ISIS, especially in areas where ISIS seeks to overthrow regimes, or areas with leaders who are involved in the Sunni-Shiite divisions within Islam. If the peaceful Muslims are a majority, they are often a silent majority. The same methods used on the French can be used on them. Often the overthrow of admittedly autocratic rulers in the name of democracy has resulted in growth of ISIS-type power and less protection for minorities.

A Different Narrative

But just how do we describe what the Parisian slaughter was? We talk of gaining control of the "narrative" so that it can be put in proper order, so that we do not become too agitated. We want to be sure so that this "violence", as it is called, does not get out of hand and challenge too many assumptions about our own world, rights, and assumptions. But ISIS does not think in these Western terms. Indeed, it

---

[1] Robert Sarah, *God or Nothing: A Conversation on Faith*, with Nicholas Diat, trans. Michael Miller (San Francisco: Ignatius Press, 2015), 139.

has contempt for them as signs of weakness. ISIS, moreover, is adept at using Western laws and institutions to achieve its own ends.

And we should remember that numbers are not necessarily a good way to think about organizations like ISIS whose power is not primarily in numbers but in will and resolve. The source of most radical change comes in the beginning in the minds of single-minded elites.

Where to begin? Eight young men carried out the Paris killings with skill and precision. Some were brothers; some came from Belgium. So far we speak of eight of them. Probably others escaped who helped plan and carry out the well-conceived operation. Seven of these men killed themselves, and one was shot before he could kill himself. They clearly intended to kill themselves after killing others if they could not get away undetected. Their deaths were included in their own plans and training. We have seen similar young men behead and slit throats of those they capture in their own controlled areas. We have become almost used to these shocking acts.

In the West, we hear questions like "This was insane! Irrational! How could anyone kill innocent people whom he did not know?" Questions like these reveal minds so conditioned that they hardly deserve to be given answers. The theologians who support these actions have no problem explaining them. We just will not hear what they tell us. There was nothing unexpected about this attack, only the time and place. When Mosul in Iraq fell to ISIS in 2014, the bishop of Mosul warned that the same blood would come to the cities of the West as came to his city. It did.[2]

---

[2] See James Schall, "Muslim Leaders Face a Dilemma", *MercatorNet*, December 2, 2014, https://www.mercatornet.com/articles/view/muslim_leaders _face_a_dilemma/15251.

Europe and the Near East are filled with thousands of young men willing to carry out similar actions in many parts of the world. Through refugee entrance points and immigration, they are already in place. Their leaders tell us that this planned slaughter in Paris was just what they will do. It is not all boasting, though some of it is. We are slow to listen to them because we have little in our minds that is realistic enough to believe them. Our schools and universities cannot examine such motivations without violating some bias. So we call them "terrorists", as if that is in any sense the name of what these men think they are.

They do not call themselves "terrorists". They call themselves true believers in what Islam formally teaches. They can point to chapter and verse, amidst conflicting chapters and verses. They laugh at us and are delighted that we do not take them seriously. They know the advantage that our ignorance and inability to say what they are gives them.

Young men persuaded by this faith blow themselves up only if they think they are accomplishing something noble and good. It is not an act of arbitrariness. Without a "cause", they would not inflict it upon themselves. They would be shocked to think that they are killing "innocent people". They reject any notion that they are killing just for the sake of killing. No, they are carrying out a "mission" assigned by Allah to all of Islam, backed, in their minds, by Qur'anic passages and a historical tradition of conquest.

No "innocent" people were found in Paris or any other country in the West (or East) except other devout Muslims who follow Allah as they do. The Parisians killed are those who are decadent with personal moral disorders prohibited by even their own laws and sacred books. They belong to the "Crusader" class that has for centuries "opposed" the destined growth of Islam in the world. The only people killed are the guilty, whether man, woman, or child.

"Why did these men", someone asked me, "choose such places as sports arenas or concert halls or bars or restaurants?" It takes little reflection to answer this question. Such places are where the brutal act would garner the most worldwide publicity for their cause. Also, in such places, they would cause fear and chaos in the civilian population, who would be more afraid of being attacked in what are supposed to be peaceful places.

The only wonder was that Notre Dame or some such church or national monument was not also a scene of killing. There is always a "next time", as the backers of these young men clearly tell us. Today, almost any target works—trains, planes, oil tanks, buses, apartment buildings, museums, barracks, police headquarters, or schools. It does not have to be the Twin Towers or the Washington Monument or Big Ben.

Why were these young men not afraid to die? Their theology tells them that they, not the ones killed, are the true martyrs. They were engaged in spreading Islam, doing good, revitalizing a historic mission. Their "noble" example will cause many other young men to join their movement, including men from France, Germany, and America.

To oppose these men, one has to be able to identify and counteract what causes them to sacrifice themselves. We do not easily make this identification. Our theories of free speech, ecumenism, and civil liberty do not allow us to study or act on the fact that such men exist. They are made into caricatures. Our ignorance is one of these men's best tools for expansion. After the French killings, many try to blame it all on "religion" or "Christianity" or retaliation of wrongs; hence, they are said to act justly. What the young men who blew themselves up wanted us to know was that they died for the noble cause of submitting the world to Allah, nothing less.

In conclusion, let me state what I think we are seeing when world attention is on Paris. From Islam's very beginning, even before there was a written Qur'an, Muhammadan armies rapidly expanded in the Near East, Africa, and Asia. They were ruthless and successful. Byzantium, Persia, Spain, and even parts of India could not resist them. The articulation of these actions came to be located in the Qur'an, but also in the record of this successful conquest of a fifth of the world by means of force.

Islam was and still is charged with submitting the whole world to Allah. This was Allah's will. After the eleventh century, this will replaced any tenuous notion that will was modified or related to *logos*, to reason. The basic tenets of Christianity were specifically denied—Trinity, Incarnation, Church. Jews and Christians could be only second-class citizens (which is still mostly the rule). The Qur'an was what it said it was, a late revelation directly from the mind of Allah that "corrected" or replaced all earlier ones.

Everything was or should be subject to Muslim law—politics, economics, family, science, and soul. Even if, say, every member of ISIS were killed, the movement would remain, only to reappear later in history to continue toward the same goal by the same methods when reread by zealous men. For its mission and what opposes it are found in the Qur'an. So long as that book is carefully and faithfully read, believers will appear and follow its admonition to subject the world to Islam, to Allah. The ISIS movement of today is not new. It is just the latest in a series of Islamic military movements, which in the past were stopped only temporarily by superior force. Islam understands power, both power of spirit and power of arms. Islam is patient, but dogged.

Is It True, or Not?

What has never really been faced, even by the Church, is the truth content, or lack of it, in the Muslim worldview with regard to the claimed truth of its understanding of God, cosmos, and man. Islam will and must always seek to expand, to submit everyone to its law. This is what "will" means. Not to do this is to deny what Islam is. This is why those young men will always appear who presently join and work to expand Islam by any means—killings, beheadings, diplomacy, war. Were it not so lethal and so intellectually incoherent, one might admire this zeal, this grandeur, yes, this "submission".

But what we witness today is not the zeal of religion in general but the inspiration of one particular religion from Mecca that sees its opportunity to expand in Europe and elsewhere by methods it has always, if we read our history, found useful. It continues the mission that was stymied in earlier centuries, especially at Tours and Vienna in battles that saved Europe.

Islam is patient, but it knows how to act suddenly when the occasion arises. If we slow it or defeat it for a time, it will rise again, so long as we do not face head-on the falsity and contradictions of the content of this faith's self-understanding.

But if we think Islam to be just another religion with no appeal to glory, it will eventually win. If we cannot give a coherent reason for this falsity, its advocates will come back again and again, because what they do is found in their faith, in their sacred book, nowhere else. Many, including Muslims, do not see this mission there. But those who do, and they are not deluded, will always be the ones who rise again, as they showed us that they could do in Paris.

18

The San Bernardino Shootings:
Another View

After almost every shooting involving a Muslim perpetrator, from 9/11 to Fort Hood to San Bernardino, we hear, from the president on down, some version of the following: "We are horrified by this inexplicable, horrendous act. Our hearts go out to the victims. This atrocity again proves the need for more gun laws." We then have a statement from some Muslim group; its spokespersons, often women, are also horrified. They had nothing to do with it; they knew nothing about it. They are concerned with retaliation. Next we have a solemn admonition from some government official assuring us that the Muslim community is peaceful, that we depend on loyal Muslims. This shooting, it is explained, was the product of a loner or two, usually a citizen of the place where the killings occurred. This insane action requires the attention of psychological health experts; ideology is mostly or entirely ignored.

Then ISIS or al-Qaida announces that it is responsible for

Adapted from "The Shootings in San Bernardino: Another View", *Catholic World Report*, December 6, 2015, http://www.catholicworldreport.com/Item /4421/the_shootings_in_san_bernardino_another_view.aspx.

the killings, whether that is actually true or not. We almost always are led to conclude that this event is just another irrational act. As with earthquakes, no real explanation exists. Such things just happen; some human beings are nutty. Since similar acts now happen every other week, if not more frequently, we have to be ready for them. We need to call in the FBI, federal agencies, more militarized police, community organizers, religious leaders, and psychiatrists. But the bottom line is that, though all religions are prone to violence, we are told that these particular happenings have nothing to do with religion, especially not Islam. They are caused by "terrorism" and "violence", as if these acts are somehow themselves independent ideological positions with no relation to the organizations that use them to foster their ends.

Is there another conceivable way to look at these events that comes closer to a more plausible explanation? The first step is to recognize that these atrocities all have a single ultimate origin. I do not mean some central command post in Syria ordering operatives today to go to Paris, tomorrow to San Bernardino, the next day to you name it, though there may be that too.

The ultimate origin is found in the history of Muslim conquests from Islam's beginning in the seventh and eighth centuries and confirmed by many passages in the Qur'an. Muslim scholars know that this jihadist approach is found within the religion. It is not an outside import; it is not an aberration. It may not be the only position found in this rambling book, but it is one that is there. This same force of spirit to convert all to Islam has abided for twelve hundred years. Yet, instead of grudgingly acknowledging it and dealing with it, we deny it exists.

Islam has no central authority. Passages in the Qur'an and its commentaries advocating holy war may be interpreted literally, symbolically, or poetically, but they are there. This jihadist inspiration always comes back to incite some Muslim believers because it is found in the sources as the only true interpretation of Islam. ISIS members insist that their religious motives be taken seriously. This earnestness is what motivates them. We insult them while at the same time playing into their hands by refusing to understand what they say and, indeed, give witness to with their lives. It is those Muslims who have died killing in Western cities—not those who are murdered—who are considered to be, yes, martyrs.

The so-called Muslim terrorists, then, do not think of themselves as Muslim terrorists. They consider themselves to be the only real followers of Muhammad. They see themselves as doing exactly what he and his first followers did in the saga of a rapid conquest of much of the African, Arab, and Middle Eastern worlds. The conquest of Europe would complete the stymied efforts at Tours and Vienna, victories that allowed Europe to remain Europe and not become Muslim much sooner. Moreover, jihadists have a perfectly intelligible explanation for what they are doing and how they are doing it. It is a sophisticated intellectual theory deftly designed to explain exactly why these "terrorist" acts are both legitimate and indeed praiseworthy in the eyes of Allah. The voluntarist metaphysics behind such reasoning is by no means unfamiliar to Western thinkers. And it is this intellectual battle that we are unwilling—or unable—to fight.

Briefly, the assigned mission of Islam is to conquer the world for Allah. Submission to Allah is the highest human good. Any means to carry it out is good if it is successful. Carrying out this mission, in this view, is a Muslim's vocation. With the reestablishment of the caliphate, this mission can now recommence. No other religions, including ones more ancient than Islam, or their symbols are allowed within Islam's conquered territories. The fact that many individual Muslims may not agree with this interpretation is irrelevant.

There are millions that do agree. But numbers are not the key factor.

Fear rules both the Muslim and Western cultures that oppose the jihadists or are their victims. This fear is kept alive by methods of warfare, shrewdly applied, that utilize modern technology but rely on old and reliable techniques. Muslim fighters learned some time ago that modern weapons are not particularly effective against them. Slitting the throats of ten Christians on international TV is more effective than weapons of mass destruction, which they would also like to possess. We see that trucks and cars are often feared means of their warfare.

Thus, tanks and bombs are not particularly effective against individual and seemingly random attacks on enemy homelands. With local passports and cell phones, small arms, homemade bombs, and knives, Muslim fighters can bring any large Western city to its knees for several days. It is something of a joke now to think that such things as the transportation safety mechanisms we have in airports make much difference. The downing of a Russian passenger plane may still happen, but attacks on schools, buses, trains, churches, or just random individuals anywhere in the world will instantly be on international news with the usual disclaimers. Bringing down passenger planes may be an obsolete means in terms of effectiveness.

As long as we choose (and it is a choice) not to identify the problem, the more it is successful and the more it will grow. That growth may indeed be the reason it is not identified. The deeper problem lies in the truth of Islam's mission to conquer the world for Allah. If Islam is true—that is, if the Qur'an is a revelation of God—then it will eventually win. Even if it is not true or from God—as I do not think that it is—even in Christian apocalyptic terms it may well win. If our view of the world is cast in terms of relativism, of diversity theory, of pacifism, we really have no clue about what is happening. One cannot but admire the logic and abiding persistence within Islam to continue its centuries-long, Allah-given mission to conquer the world.

One can speculate about why we cannot locate the source of this mission, and therefore cannot face its real attraction for its millions of followers within Islam. In no actual Muslim country is there any real freedom of religion. Whenever and wherever possible, all or part of Muslim law is established as civil law. Many Muslim countries are "peaceful" only in the sense that their governments, usually military dictatorships, keep down that radicalism that would overthrow them and is indeed overthrowing them in many places. Muslim masses wait to see who is winning. They know even within Islam that they cannot afford to be on the losing side.

The present strategy of ISIS and its followers seems clear enough. The following steps or remarks seem most plausible:

1. Gain control of governments and armies within present Islamic states.

2. Eliminate all Christian, Jewish, and related elements, including their buildings and records, from within existing Muslim states.

3. Place as many Muslims, especially young males, in European countries and other countries as possible.

4. Continue to produce large numbers of children so that demographic and democratic processes will provide increasing majorities in towns, cities, and nations.

5. Make every city and area on earth, from Mumbai to San Bernardino, the object of incidents of terror, on both a systematic and a random basis.

6. Already more than enough followers are found in most Western countries that are willing to sacrifice their lives to carry this project out in the coming years.

7. Create an atmosphere that makes it difficult to stem the Muslim conquest.

8. Undermine and convert to your use all police and military operations left remaining to oppose a final conquest.

Granted the speed of its progress, and due to the confusion and the deliberate blindness of its opposition, ISIS and its sympathizers have a reasonable hope of final success at least in Europe and possibly in America. Russia, China, and India may take longer. They will ultimately have to be dealt with. All three of these countries already have met Muslim invasions or turmoil. Their own nationalist or religious unity may prove more difficult to counter. They are, when provoked, less likely to stand by confused and relatively helpless.

And one last caveat, from Howard Kainz' essay "Christians as 'Soft Targets'": "The combination of the surrender to modernism in the 'developed world' and Christians' helpless exposure to violence and subjugation in Muslim-dominated regions leads to a possible alternative vision of Armageddon and victory: a final martyrdom of the Church."[1] The Church has no armies. Who will defend her?

---

[1] Howard Kainz, "Christians as 'Soft Targets' ", *Catholic Thing*, December 5, 2015, https://www.thecatholicthing.org/2015/12/05/christians-as-soft-targets/.

19

Novel Reflections on *Submission*

I

A former student of mine sent me a copy of the French novel *Submission*, a satirical and pointed story set in 2022. To read a novel such as this one, it is helpful to know French, the delights of French foods, cheeses, and wines, the literature of France, its religion, its geography, and its sense of style. It also helps to know the names of the streets of Paris, something of France's academic life, and the intricacies of its mind. Reading Houellebecq's novel, one realizes that all of the famous indications of the French life, both its virtues and its vices, are passing away, rather quickly, before one's very eyes—not to be replaced by complete secularism, which is already in control, but by Islam.

French words for foods and clothing have been replaced by Muslim names and phrases for a quite different cuisine and garb. The burqa-clad female students no longer bear the immediate attraction of classic, more promiscuous French coeds on the campuses and in the streets of Paris. The well-concealed Muslim girls' charms are reserved for the harem

Adapted from "Novel Reflections on *Submission*", *Catholic World Report*, December 29, 2015, http://www.catholicworldreport.com/Item/4470/novel _reflections_on_submission.aspx.

and the inner household of the legally polygamous family now supported by well-heeled French academics and businessmen who have converted to Islam. These converts are now financed by the Muslim-controlled government and by "donations" from the Saudis to foster and secure Islam in France. The more intelligent and the more powerful, in this view, simply deserve more support for the creation of larger families, which by a sort of natural selection are said to produce superior children.

If we are used to studying current events in the West, we often see them in an apocalyptic light. We see them in terms of Scripture, or perhaps of Benson's *Lord of the World*, as end times. The decadence of the West is seen as totally within the culture's own internal ambience, as if the rest of the world did not exist. It is finally judged in transcendence. It consciously rejects the revelation that, along with Greece and Rome, created the civilization known as Christendom, of which France stands almost as the heart. But since the Battle of Tours in 732, Islam has been at the gates, probing, looking for the much-prolonged conquest of Europe in Allah's name.

Houellebecq's novel does touch on these apocalyptic issues. They barely move the souls of morally compromised academics in French universities as pictured by François, the hero of this novel, a tenured professor of literature and a world-class scholar of the nineteenth-century writer J.-K. Huysmans. The most immediate end of the present civilization is not, directly at least, a divine intervention in history but a voluntary, democratic submission to Islam, a kind of inescapable hell on earth, not much less horrendous in practice than the real thing that is now so much downplayed in recent Christian thought.

This novel is a version of Jean Raspail's *Camp of the Saints*

(1973), about the invasion of the world's poor masses suddenly descending on an unprepared and prosperous Europe. They demand their equal "rights" to such prosperity. Their ideology presumes it is acquired at the expense of the poor, who really have no idea how not to be poor. They insist on keeping customs of religion and economics that never allow growth. They insist that disparity of wealth is an injustice. Obviously, this "invasion" is happening before our very eyes, but whether it is the invasion of the poor or the calculated invasion of Islam and its failures (or a combination of both) can be debated.

II

We can talk of world Islam in several ways, as Raheel Raza put it. The most fruitful one is that most Muslims believe in the Qur'an and its mission to subject the world to Allah; the world ought to be Muslim, under Muslim law. There are some ten to fifteen million men and women who belong to ISIS and its affiliates. These are the planners and the ones willing to sacrifice their lives (and ours) for their cause. Another forty or fifty million prefer to expand Islam by demographic growth and political means. They see that they can win elections and gradually transform governments that once opposed them.

Beyond these are probably four or five hundred million Muslims sympathetic to the cause but who do not much actively care until they see which side is winning. Finally, there are another half billion or so who are simply concerned with their own lives and follow without much questioning the law of Islam. The "missionary" zeal of both ISIS and the gradualists is intense and often infectious. Its root is their faith in the truth of Islamic revelation.

This novel involves the second group, the one that sees Islam primarily as a demographic and a political force that can conquer by democratic means if allowed to establish itself within democratic systems. Once inside a country, Muslims immediately set up their own enclaves, impose Islamic law, work within the system to protect themselves, and then seek to gain gradual control of political and cultural centers.

The hypothesis of this novel is that, in a close election in the near future, the party of the Muslim Brotherhood will hold the balance of parliamentary power. To rule in the French system, they join forces with the Socialist Party to defeat the Nationalist Party, the one most directly concerned with the rise of Islam within France. Once elected, when it comes to which party runs which branch of government, the Muslim Brotherhood takes not Defense, or Treasury, or Social Services, but Education. They proceed to require Muslim conversions and curricula in the schools, even in the universities.

Houellebecq's novel takes place within the sphere of the Muslim legal takeover of a French university. The French schools, while they want to retain some semblance of French tradition and international prestige, require the major offices to be in the hands of Muslim professors. Former and future faculty are offered lucrative salaries, offices, and honors in conjunction with these positions, but they have to convert. Gradually, one or another professor does this. His salary is increased; he acquires a second and a third wife. The strategists are a brilliant Muslim prime minister and a director of the university. The offers of salary and multiple wives tempt more and more faculty members. If someone does not choose to join Islam, he is bought off with a good pension, but he no longer has any place in the system.

III

It can be argued that the theme of this book is not so much
Islam as it is the corruption and the betrayal of the academic
clerics to their commitment to truth. The hero of the novel
is scholarly enough, but he has a succession of student mis-
tresses. He is unwilling or unable to commit himself to
much of anything. All through the book is a kind of nostal-
gia for home and family: "Once you reach a certain stage
of physical decline, the only relationship that really, clearly
makes sense is marriage" (150). But somehow this solution
never results in responsible action on the professor's part.

In his late forties, he sees his life as incomplete in its passing away. With the Muslim takeover of the university, he is
offered a very high academic post, which finally, after some
anguish, he accepts, and apparently converts to Islam and
receives wives and salary and security. "Submission" seems
somehow the only sensible alternative. "People really don't
care that much about their own death. What they really
worry about, their one fixation, is how to avoid physical
suffering as much as possible" (250). This view, of course,
is right out of Epicurus in ancient times, and Hobbes, Ben-
tham, and Mill in modern times.

But it is not an easy deal. The professor tries the Catholic route that his hero Huysmans took. Still, while he is
content enough in a Belgian monastery for a while, he really does not see this path as feasible for him. Both secularism and Catholicism are rejected. The title of the book
is *Submission*—this is the famous notion that the world
should be totally subject to Allah, that there is no room
for reason or logic. All things could be otherwise. We really
cause nothing. Only Allah acts. The rest is illusion. This
view means that all things, politics especially, should rule in
Allah's name. Part 5 of the novel, on an otherwise blank page,

has the following sentence from the Ayatollah Khomeini: "If Islam is not political, it is nothing."

The separation of mosque and state is a joke. Both are each other, unless corrupted by some silly notion rooted in Western Christendom about their differences. Catholicism is seen as a corruption of an original Muslim revelation. In one of the strangest misinterpretations in all of intellectual history, Christians are viewed as having corrupted the original Qur'an, instead of the Qur'an being viewed as a corruption of the Old and New Testaments—which is what it is. The theory of original revelation was concocted to justify the many incoherencies and interpretations found in the Qur'an itself.

"For the Muslim, the real enemy—the thing they fear and hate—isn't Catholicism. It's secularism. It's laicism. It's atheist materialism. They think of Catholics as fellow believers. Catholicism is a religion of the Book. Catholics are one step away from converting to Islam—that's the true, original Muslim view of Christianity" (125).

Islam is made manifest directly from the mind of Allah. Muhammad at best is just a messenger. This strange theory is absolutely necessary since all historic evidence contradicts its truth. The theory allows contradictory things to be willed by Allah. This is the voluntarism that really rules the mind of Islam.

Catholics and Muslims both argue against modern secularism. Secularism, in its turn, sees itself as a way to corrupt Islam. This novel follows a curious story in which modern secularism, in the person of the French professor, with his own moral irregularities, is converted to a Muslim way of life. He acquires three or four wives and, perhaps, some concubines. He can now do legally what he did *extra legem* as a modern professor midst sundry consenting coeds.

In this sense, Islam's real enemy is not secularism but

Catholicism, as they say, "rightly understood". This novel is, in its way, the record of the ease with which a secularist professor will find Islam more congenial and "rewarding" than Catholicism, even French Catholicism of the good kind, some of which is still about.

IV

We find many rather nice things in this book about literature and human life. "Only literature can grant you access to a spirit from beyond the grave—a more direct, a more complete, deeper access than you would have in conversation with a friend. Even in our most deepest, most lasting friendships, we never speak so openly as when we face a blank page and address an unknown reader" (5). This is well said, though perhaps more can be said for friendship. The story, including the personal story, gets us to the heart of things we are reluctant or hesitant to talk about with one another. The salvation of souls as well as minds, it might be said, includes the encounter with both Plato and Augustine, both Huysmans and Bloy, both Virgil and Dante.

We even find a sympathetic consideration of Chesterton and Belloc's distributism. If one puts into effect the distributist ideas, the cost of government would go down, labor shortages would cease, and government would not exercise the control that it does over family, education, and law. But Islam is not really distributist, and this proposal is only a quirk of a French Muslim prime minister who is guiding France to live under Islamic law.

But what in the end is the lesson of this willingness to accept Islam as the way of France—the way of the future? In one sense, it is the common materialism and decadence that both Catholics and Muslims see in the West. Catholics see it as a corruption within its own heritage, while Islam sees it as a potential threat to its own rule, even though Muslim mores and secular ones are not, on examination, so far apart. After all, one of the hopes in the West was that, if we have many Muslims come into Western countries, the relativism of the West will mitigate Islam's fanaticism. It is more likely to increase it. But the fact is that, somehow, Islam has not allowed much to interfere with its internal control of minds and polities of the billion and a half human beings who call themselves "Muslim".

The notion that Catholics are "one step away from converting to Islam" may have a historical basis. In the history of Islam, its conquest of once-Christian lands did see gradual conversions once Islamic law was enforced over a period of time. In Islamic states one's choice is (1) die, (2) convert, or (3) accept second-class citizenship and pay the required taxes. Only Christian remnants survived in Muslim lands. These remnants are now being killed or driven out of their ancient lands. In exile, they find themselves not recognized by modern Western governments as anything different from the Muslims also flooding Europe for often quite different reasons, one of which is no doubt the conversion of Europe to Islam.

To the tired French academic, who converts to Islam for its rewards and because he has no place else to go, "submission" seems to be both a "scientific" and the simplest cultural alternative. "Submission" is, after all, what "Islam" means; the book's title was well chosen. To mindlessly submit solves a lot of problems if we simply accept the Muslim law and do not worry about anything but to observe it till death. If Allah does everything, we need not worry about "doing" anything, or being at all concerned with what we do. Whatever happens, whatever it is, is Allah's will. "Submission", then, is not understanding or vision but all that is left to us.

20

Realism and Islam

I

Political realism, long associated with Augustine, constrains us to consider what Machiavelli later recommended to us— namely, to look at what men *do* do and not at what they *ought* to do. Machiavelli thought that if men did what they *ought* to do, they would not survive the onslaughts and cunning of those who did whatever they had power to do. However, Augustinian realism did not, as in the case of Machiavelli, justify this careful look at what men *do* do as a reason to deny the distinction between good and evil so that any means could be used to accomplish men's purposes.

The "realistic" look was "realistic" for Augustine precisely because good and evil *were* included in the look itself, in the reality as seen. To see and act on the reality of good or evil is to see reality in its fullest dimensions. Practical truth, in terms of acting according to an accurate description of what is there, is the first principle of realism as well as of political action. Thus, Jacques Maritain could rightly maintain in the Augustinian tradition that "justice, brains, and strength" need not be separated. They belong together. Or, to refer obliquely to Lord Acton, the lack of power can

Adapted from "Realism and Islam", *Catholic World Report*, April 17, 2016, http://www.catholicworldreport.com/Item/4731/realism_and_islam.aspx.

also corrupt absolutely. Not to possess and to use responsible power in defense of what is right is itself an evil, a cowardice.

With this background in mind, we recall recent events from 9/11, the bombings in Spain, England, Mumbai, Bali, Fort Hood, San Bernardino, Paris (twice), Lahore, and Brussels, not to mention the persecutions and beheadings in Pakistan, Iraq, Yemen, Nigeria, Libya, Somalia, Chad, and Syria, and the Sunni-Shiite intra-Islam battles. What is the most plausible way to judge such continuing violence and its origins? To make this assessment, we have to acknowledge that Islam, in principle, is actually and potentially violent, and has been throughout its entire history. The basic reason for violence is obedience to the law of Allah, not love for violence itself.

On the basis of evidence and theory, we cannot conclude from the fact that Islam is a religion that therefore it is not violent or is so only by abuse of its own founding. It is possible for a religion to espouse violence. (Were this not so, we would have to exclude many key passages in the Old Testament itself.) We cannot obscure what is in Islam and affirmed to be there by Muslims themselves. Realism means that we can and should call what happens by its proper name. It also means that, if we cannot or will not make this proper naming, we are not realistic. We will inevitably suffer the consequences of our failure to state the truth of what is there.

These things are said not to promote counterviolence against Muslims or to justify Muslim violence against others. Rather, these things are said to respect Islam's insistence that all those inside and outside of its enclosure be subject to Islamic law. Whether we like it or not, this vision of world rule that is proper to Islam can be called only "religious" in nature. It is rooted in and promoted as a worship of the god called Allah. Not to take this wording seriously is unrealistic. The Muslims who claim that they can read their religious texts as if such violence is not advocated and justified may be applauded for trying to mitigate the historic record. But the fact is that those who see this violence as essential to the religion have the better side of the argument and are the better witnesses to what historic Islam stands for.

II

What is argued here, then, is not meant to be unfairly critical of Islam. On the contrary, it is written with considerable admiration for the zeal, consistency, and effectiveness displayed over the centuries by Islamic armies and law. And while it may be politically incorrect to state these things, they need to be stated and are in fact the truth—things that both Muslims and non-Muslims need to hear and consider. The designated and determined goal of the conquest of the world for Allah has been reinvigorated again and again in world history from the time of Muhammad in the seventh century. These revivals and expansions, which have been only temporarily halted by superior counterforce, have roots in the Qur'an itself and in its commentaries.

What we witness today, much to our surprise, is but another step in the historic world mission that Islam envisions for itself as the will of Allah, a goal that inspires the real and recurrent vigor that is found in Islam's history. The reason we do not call it what it is lies not in Islam but in our own very different concepts of philosophy, religion, and law. In this sense, it is our own culture that often prevents us from being ourselves political realists.

Many believing Muslims, likely more than we are willing to admit, are tired and frustrated at having their religion's principles denied. Outside observers are unwilling to believe or imagine that what Muslim advocates say about themselves, both in their founding texts and in their historic actions, is true. World conquest over time is what they hold must be achieved.

In other words, whether they be Muslim or otherwise, many people refuse to acknowledge that violence is proposed and carried out in the name of Islam. Outside Islam, it is called by the peculiar word "terrorism". It is rarely called what it is, namely, a religious endeavor to conquer the world as an act of piety. Muslims, in this central tradition, are not "terrorists" just for the fun of it. That is insulting and resented. They practice what we call "terror" because they see themselves carrying out the will of Allah, even sometimes to their own death in doing so. Those who, in the process, kill "infidels"—that is, non-Muslims or Muslims who do not accept true Islam—are considered to be "martyrs" to the cause of Islam. Only if Islam is not true can these ritual killings be seen as the objective evil that they are.

A subtle philosophic theory (called "voluntarism") purports to justify this usage of what we call terror for religious purposes. The principle of contradiction cannot hold in a "revelation" that contains, in its texts, contradictory commands, as does the Qur'an. Allah then must become pure will, not bound by *logos*, or reason. Hence, Allah is not limited by any distinction of good and evil. The Muslim blasphemy laws that threaten with death anyone who violates this claim arise from this source.

Allah's mandate to Islam is progressively to subject the world to his will and to the law based on it. Terror will end and true "peace" will result only when all are submissive to Allah and live under Muslim law in all its details. What we outside of Islam call acts of violence are considered within it to be the carrying out of Allah's will. Gruesome beheadings of Christians, however innocent, are seen as acts of justice. They are acts of "virtue" in this sense. The people who cannot understand this religious charge given to Islam, whether they be themselves Muslim or not, are themselves both unrealistic and dangerous. Their own presuppositions prevent them from recognizing and judging the real issue. These presuppositions also prevent them from doing anything effective to hinder this expansion of Islam into Europe, Asia, Africa, and America.

III

Back in 1975, I wrote an essay in the *Modern Age* entitled "On the Teaching of Ancient and Medieval Political Theory".[1] The gist of this essay was that unless we understand the content and history of religions—their truth claims and aberrations—we will be unable to see the actual forces that swirl through the political world. An education that lacks a proper and accurate study of the theology peculiar to each different religion is not really an education. It could not prepare anyone to deal with a world in which religions, in their differences, are a reality. Both in Europe and America in the last half century or longer, this sanitized education is what students have been given. With it, most citizens are simply not equipped to face the forces now reappearing in the world. Indeed, even to propose a realistic look at Islam, as is proposed here, is almost everywhere forbidden and excluded from any consideration, however valid the analysis.

---

[1] *Modern Age*, Spring 1975, 157–66. Available at the Intercollegiate Studies Institute website, https://isistatic.org/journal-archive/ma/19_02/schall.pdf.

This neglect of or hostility to religion has come back to haunt us. We have lumped all religions together as illusions or myths. They are to be defanged and wholly subject to state power. Our political, academic, and cultural leaders cannot comprehend what is going on, either when a whole Western civilization loses its faith and moral standards or when Islam reawakens to the implications of its own faith and its vision of world conquest. The two—the loss of faith in the West and the rise of Islam—are connected. The decline of the birthrate and civil undermining of the family in the West is one thing. Muslim immigration or invasion has engulfed this same area. Muslims, especially young males, did not seek power and prosperity in other adjoining Muslim lands. The expansion of Islam was justified also by its charge of moral decadence against the West.

We see well-equipped but unmotivated modern armies, with inept and unseeing political leadership, outfought by young armed zealots in pickup trucks who can, with their followers, threaten every train station and public building in Europe, Africa, Asia, and America. As they planned, they have managed to turn the whole world into a battleground of fear. The cry "Allah be praised!" is heard after every act of destruction. It is quite clear by now, or should be, that no non-Muslim cultural artifacts—be they books, buildings, statues, or paintings—will be allowed to exist. They are seen to be contrary to Allah's will, no matter what they are or when they were created. In this sense, the Pyramids, the Buddhist statues, the library in Timbuktu, the Vatican, the monasteries in the deserts, Canterbury, the towers in New York, the kosher markets in Paris, and the airports in Brussels are equally subject to destruction. Everything must be protected because everything is now threatened.

Not only are individual Christians eradicated, but so are

the statues of their saints. The reason for this destruction is religious. Such things ought not to exist. We have here a literal application of the belief that nothing should be allowed public or private space that does not correspond with strict Muslim beliefs. Provisional tolerance of Christians and Jews if they accept second-class citizenship and pay heavy fines is merely temporary until the conquest is complete. Such zealous destruction to do the will of Allah, in other words, is considered to be an act of piety. If someone is going to oppose such acts, it cannot be done on the grounds of opposition to "terror" or that it is unreasonable. Ultimately, it depends, as Augustine learned with the Donatists, on conversion and rejection of the theology that justifies it.

IV

Whether Islam, in its origins, is a rereading of Jewish, Nestorian, and Christian texts (as it probably is) can be disputed. First, Islam claims to be a literal revelation of what is in the mind or being of Allah. In this sense, what is in the text must always remain in the text. It cannot be changed or "reinterpreted" to leave out those multiple passages that propose and justify violence in the name of the expansion of this religion. This advocacy of violence, which has been practiced in Islam from its seventh-century beginning, has a purpose. This purpose is, ultimately, religious and pious. Whether the Muslim notion of "heaven", where its martyrs go, is primarily this-worldly or transcendent, can also be disputed. In any case, the concept of heaven is very earthy sounding. This picture of paradise is not, as such, an argument against its truth.

The message contained in the Qur'an is that the world

should bow in submissive worship to Allah. This purpose abides and recurs over the centuries because it is there in the text. Men may temporarily neglect its zealous pursuit, but the text itself always contains the mission for others to find and pursue. There will always be those who realize that the mission of world conquest in the name of Allah is not complete. This realization is why, so long as it exists unrefuted, the Qur'an will always produce what we call "terrorists". What we see now is little different from what has been seen throughout the centuries wherever Islam is found.

In this view, the world is divided into an area of peace and an area of war. The former is where the law of Allah rules politically, religiously, and culturally, where no other philosophy or faith has any right to be present. All signs of alien religion, art, artifact, and people are eliminated through forced conversion or destruction. Sometimes, Christians and Jews can be allowed to stay alive provided that they accept second-class citizenship and pay taxes. This situation, in practice, is the basic constitutional rule in all existing Muslim states, even in those that reject ISIS or other violent approaches to eventual conquest of the world. Once Islam has conquered, it has always followed the same principles. In its history, certain famous battles have turned back Muslim conquests for a time, sometimes for centuries. But this relative inertness is only on the surface. As long as the book exists, its goals will again and again inflame prophets, imams, politicians, and young men to recommence the conquest of the rest of the world.

In conclusion, what is argued here in terms of political realism is that we must understand the religious nature of Islamic expansion and the methods used to achieve it. Trying to abstract this motivation from the soul of this particular religion, which is, on this score, unlike most others, only makes it impossible to describe what in fact is going on in the mind of the adversary that is Islam. Wars are first fought in minds—and this is a war. It is not World War III; rather, it is an extension of the wars that Muhammad first launched against Byzantium, Persia, Syria, eventually North Africa, and even India, Spain, and the Balkans.

The Muslim protagonists of today realize how close they were several times in the past to conquering Europe as the next step in world conquest. What they see today is a very realistic opportunity to succeed where their ancestors failed. They, though idealists, are also (often unlike ourselves) realists. That is, they see what our minds really hold. And they see that those minds are largely empty of what really counts in this world: a true conception of God. Islam's only fault is that of choosing a false understanding of the real God. Aside from this "small" issue, one cannot help but admire, and fear, a blind faith that so abides over time and in almost every place without the real presence of the *logos*, whose incarnate presence in the world is explicitly denied.

21

Orlando in Hindsight

I

As it turns out, the killings in Orlando were not what they seemed to be or what too many wanted them to be—that is, simply a random act of "hatred" caused by a deranged young man with no real relation to any religion. Or, perhaps, if we insist on relating it to religion, then, as some prelates argued or suggested, all religions are equally guilty. Even if the killings were by a "loner", he was an active radical Muslim killer whose rationale was from this tradition. The killings remain one more careful, calculated move of ISIS to seize on every opportunity to continue a grand, too-long-delayed, and neglected plan to undermine the stability of every non-Muslim country in the world. The Islamic countries that oppose ISIS can be dealt with later. In pursuing this goal, Islamic advocates think grandly. Opponents to it often think so narrowly that they cannot understand what is happening to them in the world.

A coherent approach to a historic mission is only a recently realized possibility on the part of many in modern Islam. In this view, things are now moving quickly in the

Adapted from "Orlando in Hindsight", *Catholic World Report*, June 24, 2016, http://catholicworldreport.com/Item/4874/Orlando_in_Hindsight.aspx.

right direction. Opportunities must be and are being seized. We see thousands of unidentified Muslims, usually young men of fighting age, continue to pour into Europe and now America under the guise that they are just like other needy immigrants. Be it noted that they do not "pour" into other nearby Muslim states, where they presumably would be right at home. No pressing need can be found to conquer what is already conquered.

Besides, Muslim lands are among the poorest in the world, so no reason exists to flee to them unless for reasons of political control. Their poverty is almost directly related to their religious culture with its ideas about the direct causality of all things by Allah. Moreover, when Islam emigrates, it takes its culture with it. It transplants it into Europe or into the New World. Islam does not often assimilate; that is an alien idea. It thereby denies and undermines all the presuppositions of Western liberal politics that insist on seeing it as just another religion. In new lands, when it settles there, it reproduces what it brought with it. It gradually imposes its culture on others when it can, even by sophistic use of "democratic" means. Several Muslim groups are now realizing that this "democratic" way may be a faster way to achieve their end than the violent way. But both options remain open.

An American-born member of a politically active Afghani family showed up as the next in a long, mostly forgotten succession of such attacks by similar unknowns in this and other countries. Such an act cannot be explained in psychological, antigay, or "terrorism-for-the-sake-of terrorism" terms. Each individual Muslim killer, including the man in Orlando, ritually affirms his loyalty to Islam. Many in the West refuse to believe that such a religious motive could be serious. But this unwillingness only reveals an ignorance of Islam and the paucity of much Western thought.

This or any other terrorist has good religious reasons in Muslim tradition and scripture to kill non-Muslims. This affirmation is accepted as such by ISIS and other Muslim groups even if the killing is committed by an individual not directly commanded by or affiliated with a Muslim group. In many ways, it is more effective for the ISIS cause if no direct connection is made.

The attacks are, in one way or another, the result of an "inspired" politico-religious belief that incites such acts to put the Islamic way of life into effect. Such actions have been going on more or less successfully since the beginnings of Islam in the seventh century. By any standards, Islam has been an enormously successful endeavor. It usually expanded and conquered by quick military or terrorist strikes. But now many Muslim leaders also recognize the importance of demographic growth to gain the religion's ultimate goal of the eventual submission of every nation to Allah. But the use of terror is not underestimated. It also is relied on as a direct means to undermine the stability of modern cities and economies.

Such is the poverty of our politically correct educational systems, aided by governmental policies, that we generally have few intellectual tools available to us that enable us to comprehend the persistence of an idea over centuries, one capable of being carried on to a logical conclusion in historic time. And this mission predates Western Hegelianism. Islam is what it is. "May Allah be praised!" is not just a slogan. The obtuseness in understanding is perhaps one of the greatest self-imposed blindnesses ever shown forth by supposedly rational leadership. But this blindness too can be explained, even in biblical terms. We do not see what we choose, for our own reasons, not to see.

The rise of Islam may be made more feasible by the modern decline in reason and in Christianity's understanding of its own revelation. But opportunism is not the heart of the matter. Islam proposes itself as the successor—or better, as the replacement—of both reason and Christianity. But it also proposes itself to and seeks to expand in other cultures, to India and to China, as the way Allah should be worshipped in these places also. In India, Islam gained much ground by conquest but came to a standstill when India finally resisted. The China opening has begun, though China probably presents a much more difficult task than the West.

II

I write these comments as an admirer of the Islam of ISIS. I do not, of course, admire what it does in terms of terror or destruction. While Islam is, as I judge it, a false religion, it is held by true believers who are much more accurate in their reading of their own classical texts than any of their critics. The struggles within Islam itself between Sunni and Shiite interpretations of Islam are not, as such, disagreements about these ends or even about the means to obtain them. What is going on cannot simply be explained in terms of modern political theory, by psychology, by economics, or by social science. It can be explained only by taking what the Qur'an and Muslim tradition say of Islam and the means by which the religion can propagate itself.

A report from Judicial Watch (June 15, 2016) recounted the arrest in New Mexico of a Muslim woman coming out of Mexico who just happened to have in her possession the blueprints of the gas system in that area of New Mexico. Her motive seems to have been to further the cause of Islam, not to repair gasworks in New Mexico. We must wonder how many blueprints of various electrical grids, gas lines, power lines, rail lines, airports, highways, bridges, tunnels, school campuses, churches, sports complexes, TV stations, or government buildings are already in the hands of ISIS members and sympathizers. We should not think that they do not know how to read them. Many of the terrorists are well educated and well trained.

To assume that any place in Europe, America, or Canada is safe, at this stage of the game, is naive. In every major and minor city in the world, we can likely find ISIS sympathizers who are willing to sacrifice their lives for this cause either when ordered to do so or when they see an opportunity. We have exacerbated this situation ourselves by failing to understand Islam and what men and women will do to foster it. We have major Muslim centers in every major city, often financed by Saudi money; we know little of what goes on in them. What we do know is often more than unsettling. President Obama has refused to name the enemy in any but vague, general terms. His policies have been almost invariably favorable to the Muslim cause in one form or another.

After Orlando, columns by Mary Jo Anderson, Carl E. Olson, Maureen Mullarkey, Pat Buchanan, Andrew McCarthy, George Rutler, Joseph Pearce, and a host of others have pretty well gotten it right. The president of the United States, the Democratic candidate, even Mr. Trump, much of the press, many bishops, college professors, and foreign politicians have it wrong. To acknowledge that it is what it is would be to admit that practically speaking their whole intellectual and political life has been wrongly directed. And it has been. We keep hearing pleas for them to "wake up", but it is not happening. ISIS and Muslim Brotherhood thinkers, each in their own way, pretty well know this refusal to take them at their word and take comfort in it. They know that their likelihood of being caught is slim if their enemies will not see and understand.

It has long been noted by some perceptive thinkers that Islam will expand, and rapidly expand, if it is not stopped by superior force. This is a truth that pacifist-minded people do not like to hear. I also think that Islam's ideas and texts need directly to be confronted. They cannot be simply set aside and unexamined as too controversial to talk about, analyze, and criticize. Since almost all versions of Islam react angrily or even violently to any fundamental criticism of its basic positions, we have backed off on prudential or diplomatic grounds to talk only of things "about which everyone could agree". It is what we do not agree with in Islam that needs to be talked about most. This delicate approach has not worked and never will. But the actual expansion of Islam, whenever and wherever it was able to increase, has been stopped only by superior force. Superior force is usually only a passing thing. Indeed, modern military force may not be able to stop the kind of expansion that depends not on superior military hardware but on direct killings and self-sacrifice of true believers. The brutal beheading of Coptic Christians in Libya was much more terrifying than the counterpicture of helicopter gunships shooting at ISIS fighters in the desert.

There is only one good reason why Europe is not Muslim today (though it probably will be Muslim eventually, through its own political choices). This non-Muslim Europe is the result of two great battles: one at Tours in the eighth century and one at Vienna in the seventeenth. The historic, self-defensive efforts of European powers to eliminate the constant danger of Islamic attack failed when Europe could not permanently retake the Holy Land and Byzantium. This counterattack failed because of superior Muslim force. But Europe also did not understand the importance of knowing what Islam was. It was this closing off of lands south and east of Europe that gave rise to the inner European development of modern states, cultures, and economies.

Likewise, most Islamic bastions in the Near East and in Africa were controlled by European powers from the Napoleonic Wars in the early 1800s to the end of World War II. What is interesting, if not frightening, about this record is that Islam proved largely impervious to change. After accepting voluntarism in theology, Islam could produce no science. Most of the science that was in earlier ages of Islam came from scholars who were originally Christian or Persian. In this aspect, it has not much changed. Its oils, the source of much of its riches, is mostly a result of economies and technologies that do not originate in Islam. The notion that it ought to change is not an Islamic idea. Its idea is closer to the view that it ought not to change. Islam in its closed family and community traditions manages effectively by a combination of faith, persuasion, and force to keep its masses loyal to itself. The Muslim idea is, again, that it ought not to change its essentials. It ought to set up and impose Sharia law everywhere. It ought to remain true to Allah. It turns out that they seem to have the better part of the argument. Their will to resist change is stronger than our will either to change them or to prevent them from changing us.

The following comment of an Englishman in a recent *Financial Times* makes the point:

> It is more likely that ISIS is modelling itself on the Islamist military strategy of the 7th and 8th centuries. It was then easy to offer stunned opponents the choice of conversion to Islam, death, or the adoption of *dhimmi* status, and so achieve the ultimate objective—the continuous expansion of the area subject to sharia law. Modern authorities may

care to note that this strategy had one weakness: it failed when the initial violence was met with a robust military response which demonstrated a level of determination even greater than that of the Islamists.[1]

This is well said and true to experience and theory. Islam must expand or suspect that Allah has willed against it by Muslim defeats. It is part of the logic of its theology.

III

Orlando—like San Bernardino, Fort Hood, the Spanish trains, the Paris concert hall, and the Mumbai hotel—will soon be forgotten or minimized in the light of ever-new events of the same order. Radical Islam is now a two-pronged force: the ISIS side and the Muslim Brotherhood side. Both have the same goal. The first relies on more direct military and terrorist methods. The latter does not shun these means but finds that a more effective way to gain control is through the shrewd use of democratic methods. Both are aware of the demographics that Islam has over cultures that have been contracepting themselves out of existence. This decline in willingness even to have children in any significant numbers is not the result of Muslim thought, which, in its odd way with multiple wives, is pronatal, however disordered a polygamous family may be for men, women, and their children. In this sense, numbers count. Islamic thinkers have every right to expect that numbers are in their favor. Several European countries can expect to be predominately Muslim in ten to thirty years.

---

[1] David J. Critchley, "Islamists' Centuries-Old Strategy Has a Weakness", letter to *Financial Times*, May 12, 2016.

Aristotle had already said that large changes in population and culture would transform any existing regime into something else. The American regime, in particular, has doggedly maintained that it could welcome anyone into its country. It took this position on the assumption that certain basic ideas about human nature were agreed on. Most of the immigrants, until recent years, came from the same broad European Christian culture that had much in common. It was not until the twenty-first century that America's political culture decided that there was no human nature to agree about and that religion was not relevant.

Everyone had a "right" to his own view of the cosmos. The effects of this relativism are straightforward. All individuals and institutions must accept the principle of relativism to continue in the public order. What is unique about Islam is that it has been able to use the principles of relativism to secure a place within the legal world that has no means to reject it other than to call it "terrorism". But in a relativist world, even terrorism has a theoretic place. If there are no real standards, it is difficult to see on what grounds it can be excluded.

What Islam seems to understand more clearly than those who welcome it into their presence is that it does not accept either the Christian or the relativist premises of the culture. All factions within Islam positively reject them. It does not follow from this rejection that what Islam does hold is therefore correct. It is in fact just another danger from another direction, one rooted in ideas unique to itself. The opposite of truth is usually not just one error but many. Islam, however, has the advantage in being able to close itself off from the surrounding social and political order, especially from one that will not confront it on the grounds of its own presumed truth. If we deal with Islam only as just another "right" among other equally indefensible "rights", it will thrive in a liberal environment. It will vote en bloc for its own interests. The advantage that the surrounding relativist culture gives to Islam is enormous. In a way, Islam has the best of both worlds. That is, it can operate as "legitimate" within and demand protection of democratic systems that are based on willed "rights". It can also attack such a system as corrupt from both the inside and the outside with those ISIS-type forces that maintain that, when using these forces, their understanding of Islam is the correct one.

IV

Meantime, in conclusion, Iraqi forces finally seem to be having some success in retaking cities that ISIS, with much publicity and violence, had taken over. This scene is again a reminder that much of the violence that we see in the Islamic world is directed by Muslims against each other. We see the Sunni-Shiite division, the Wahhabi influence, the de facto frontiers of Islamic states, the claim that a single caliphate has been established, Hamas, al-Qaida, and the Muslim Brotherhood. Governments in Turkey, Iran, Egypt, Indonesia, Nigeria, and Saudi Arabia, as well as those in the smaller Muslim states like Yemen, Qatar, Kuwait, and others, are themselves under internal and external pressure to adopt the ISIS form of Islam. Many would prefer to let the Muslims fight it out among themselves. The complications of internal Muslim politics and controversies are no doubt bewildering.

It does not take many people to cause a revolution in fact, though it does require ideas. That Europe and America could be seen as targets of Muslim rule seems at first sight preposterous. Yet, a method, an opportunity, and an organization have arisen upon the premise that the conquest of good parts, if not all, of Europe and America is possible. Islam understands that its enemy is itself confused and bears within itself as many diverse and conflicting currents as are found within Islam. But this lack of any unified faith in the West is precisely why it is seen to be vulnerable by those whose faith in Allah is absolute. Islam is a shrewd religion that grew by the violence that is part of its sacred book and its heritage. Terror need not always be used; some Muslims oppose it. But it can be and often is most effective for its own ends. It is not contradictory to the understanding of Allah in the Muslim mind. Islam has not repudiated its own heritage. It is bound by it. It has in our time seen the possibility of universalizing it to subject the whole world to Allah. We continue to think this hope is naive or impossible. But the brains behind ISIS and the Muslim Brotherhood are right. The opportunity is there for the taking. As yet, they do not see any force or ideas sufficient to deter them.

To look back retrospectively on Orlando is to see it as one more successful example of what one person can do if he has a mission and a worldview to justify it. The Orlando killer was not alone. He was a true believer, and other believers in the mission of Islam inspire him. Neither he nor any of his predecessors or future companions are to be explained by psychology, economics, or sociology. They are to be explained by taking their word for what they are doing. If the president of the United States or the British prime minister, the media, the professors, the clerics cannot or will not understand this reality, we cannot blame ISIS and its friends. They are also realists who understand where ideas and reality meet, sometimes on a battlefield in Iraq, sometimes in a nightclub in Orlando.

ISIS, the Muslim Brotherhood, and the Saudis may lose. But, as of now, they have a good chance of winning. Whether a victory of Islam in subjecting the world to Allah would be a victory for the world or a disaster is best answered when the conquest has succeeded. And then no other answer would be allowed in this world but "Allah be praised!" One last thing is clear: Christians and other non-Muslims in any existing Muslim state are still denied religious freedom, full civil rights, full freedom of speech. They remain second-class citizens. Most Christians are now out of many Muslim states. Orlando, in other words, is an isolated incident that forces us to see what is happening. Its second lesson is that many, even in the highest places, refuse to see. In this, they are not innocent.

22

The Two Truths Revisited

Considerable turmoil has been generated by a Vatican-related tweet.[1] It proposed that two plus two equals four in science, but in theology the sum could equal five. This "possibility" of five was not exactly new or even startling, except perhaps for its source. The two-truth theory has its uses, no doubt.

Machiavelli famously proposed that human freedom would be exponentially expanded if at least the prince rid himself of the distinction between good and evil. In effect, he proposed a version of this theory that is usually associated with the Muslim thinkers Averroës and al-Ghazali. The "truth" of politics and the "truth" of morality are both true. We affirm that evil should not be done. But sometimes it should be done. In that case, evil becomes good.

The two-truth theory held, in its purest form, that a truth of reason and a truth of religion or theology could contradict each other. But both are still true. The Aristotelian tradition held that this situation could not be the case. One view

---

Adapted from "The Two Truths Revisited", *Catholic Thing*, January 31, 2017, https://www.thecatholicthing.org/2017/01/31/the-two-truths-revisited/.

[1] See Carlo Lancellotti, "Fr. Spadaro's Math", *First Things*, January 19, 2017, https://www.firstthings.com/blogs/firstthoughts/2017/01/fr-spadaros -math.

was right; the other was wrong. Reason cannot contradict reason, be it human or divine.

That is what reason means. A thing cannot be and not be at the same time in the same way in the same circumstances. This is called a "first principle". It is so called because nothing can be clearer from which to deduce the principle. We affirm that something exists. At the same time, we implicitly deny that it is something else.

The average man may not be carried away by these seemingly esoteric reflections. In truth, they are quite fascinating. Some ancient Greeks and Romans dickered with such thoughts, as did later the followers of Occam. The people who, on a large scale, first utilized the proposition that a truth of reason and a truth of theology could contradict each other were seeking to defend Allah.

Why did Allah need defending? It was because of a book he is said to have written manifesting his mind. The men who developed these notions were pious men. They were sharp enough to see that, in a book said to be revealed, contradictory claims were made. Something had to be done to cover the reputation of the god against evident inconsistencies.

The solution that such thinkers came up with, when spelled out, was remarkable. They did not deny that contradictions existed. They said that Allah could will one thing on Tuesday and its opposite on Wednesday. The latest affirmation is always the binding one, but it can change tomorrow. In thinking these notions through, men found that things became ever more complicated.

If the will of Allah could affirm one thing on Tuesday and its opposite on Wednesday, he could do the same thing with all the laws of nature. Since truth is grounded not in *logos* but in *voluntas*, the only way we could know that the sun will arise in the morning is if God wills it and we believe it. He could will that it not come up. These presuppositions mean that we cannot really rely on nature for anything.

In this perspective, nobody but Allah does anything. It is blasphemy to suggest otherwise. If we make a fortune one day but lose it the next, in both cases it is solely the will of Allah. Our enterprise has nothing to do with it. Our skills or lack thereof mean nothing. Science cannot really exist in such a world. No incentive is found to investigate nature if it can be otherwise at every instant.

A Christian and a secularist version of this theory exist, particularly in moral and political philosophy. Nature is evaporated of any content. The difference between Islam and this Western view is not so great when we come right down to it. One theory makes Allah's will responsible for what goes on, so that whatever happens is Allah's will. The other theory places the will in the individual person so that he is subject not to any ordered nature but only to his own will.

The Machiavellian version is simply "What the prince (democracy) wills is the law", to cite a Roman law adage, later cited by Aquinas. In a conflict of individual and collective will, the latter almost always wins, as Hobbes saw.

Why are two-truth theories proposed? Almost invariably they arise to justify what cannot be justified in reason, including the reason of faith. When some position, said to belong to revelation, can be justified only by denying that the Divinity is bound by reason, by *logos*, we know we are dealing with the two-truth issue.

Ultimately, the justification of heresy always involves, in its logic, the denial of reason. Or to put it the other way around, when we see that what is called "revelation" needs to resort to arbitrary will, divine or human, to justify itself, we know that we have reached incoherence.

23

Manchester, London, and
the Goals of Islam

I

A friend was recently in Paris waiting to visit Notre Dame. Suddenly sirens, police, and chaos were everywhere. A young Muslim was shot trying to knife a guard. The place could not have been more symbolic. It fleetingly recalls what happened in Santa Sofia in May 1453. In 2014 the archbishop of Mosul, after his church and city had been destroyed, warned that the same thing would soon happen in Europe. It has begun. We now expect increasing "incidents".

Indeed, our getting used to them follows our not being willing identify the cause. Armies and police are mostly useless in the present context. They can only react to an enemy who can act anywhere. If, under the rubric of compassion, humanitarianism, aiding refugees, or alleviating poverty, we bring into a society masses of people whose understanding of God and man is not ours, we can expect trouble. The question then becomes: Do they become like us, or do we become like them? The incidents in London, then Man-

Adapted from "Manchester, London, and the Goals of Islam", *Catholic World Report*, June 11, 2017, http://www.catholicworldreport.com/2017/06 /11/manchester-london-and-the-goals-of-islam/.

chester, then Paris, then London again are not isolated. We dare not ask, "Why are they not?"

Dealing with Islam is a function of understanding Islam. Islam is a book and a history. They belong together. It is a religion that is a politics. The billion and a quarter Muslims on this planet today are divided into some fifty separate, yet not-so-separate, political entities. These entities now have no universal caliphate but would like one. Islam has no central authority. Muslims are also divided into Sunnis and Shiites, plus a few other groups. They often war against each other.

"What is Islam?" yields many opinions. What follows here is a minority opinion. It seeks to state the facts and the theory that explain what is happening in our time. "Islam versus the world" is a better summation than "Islam's place in the world". Briefly, Islam has no settled "place" in the world until the world is simply Islam with no other option available. Islam is in turmoil with itself as long as what is not Islam exists and flourishes.

In its own terms, Islam has a noble mission: namely, to submit the world to Allah. This goal has been on its horizon since the religion's beginning in the seventh century, when such an accomplishment seemed impossible. Islam needs to be roused up from time to time. We live in an era of its renewed self-rousing. Yet, nothing can be found in philosophy, revelation, or natural religion that can justify it. We can only explain it. Islam, at least from the eleventh century, in an effort to justify its many internal contradictions before reality, developed a voluntarist understanding of Allah whereby anything could be justified, even the opposites of good and evil, truth and falsity. To uphold this option, no basic questioning is allowed. Force, in various forms—not reason—upholds the doctrine embodied in the Qur'an and the culture it inspires.

Voluntarism means that no objective order is found in human or natural things. Everything that we see could be otherwise. The cause of anything that happens is the un-grounded will of Allah. He is not ruled by *logos*, reason. Hence, he is not and cannot be limited by the distinction between good and evil. If Allah were so limited, he would, in this view, not be all-powerful and therefore would not be divine. Thus, in Muslim eyes, any effort to submit Allah to reason is a betrayal of his omnipotence. The notion that something is contradictory has no meaning in a voluntarist system. The planet is divided between a world of peace— that is, what is already controlled by Islam—and a world with which Islam is at war. Universal peace means nothing less than the elimination of a sphere of war—that is, the elimination of a place where Islam does not impose its law on all existing people and their cultures.

My view here is intended to be not polemic but descrip-tive. It might well be wrong in various details. But it is a defense of Islam in the sense that it is philosophically proper and necessary to state what Islam is; it is also a critique of why its continuing expansion is a judgment on the blind-ness and ineptness of those opposing it. Given a choice, no doubt, these latter would not decide to become Muslim, even if confronted with the famous Islamic alternative that so many have faced in the past twelve centuries: death or conversion. On the other hand, they evidently do not see what their future will be if Islam succeeds, as it well might, in expanding to other areas or to the whole of the world.

In the "beginning" in Western thought, to recall both Aristotle and John's Gospel, the world is as it is. It does not exist as the result of some human establishment. Knowing that the world exists not of ourselves, we seek to find a cause both of why it is and of why it is this way, not that way. In Islam, the beginning and the end could be otherwise with equal grandeur. Allah could make anything the opposite of what it is. There is no stability in things, since, should Allah so will it, anything could be its opposite. Nature yields not order but arbitrariness. This realization paralyzes the Muslim mind. This is why, in Islam, submission is nobler than reason.

Reason supposes that God wanted rational beings also to know Him and freely to love Him. Submission presupposes that we can know nothing. Our only alternative is to accept whatever happens and bow unquestioningly because no reasons are available or possible. We have here the grandeur of complete helplessness. Our only input is to accept it, whatever it is. The primary mission of Islam is to subject the rest of the world, for its own good, to this same view and practice. When this happens, there will be peace on earth.

II

As each bombing, shooting, knifing, or truck-crashing incident comes along—whether in Europe, Asia, Africa, or the Americas—much of the world comprehends it as it did the previous bombing, and the knifing before that, and the incident before that. That is, it officially treats it as an individual problem of some usually "fanatical" or otherwise-confused youth acting on his own. Officials hope against hope that it was not the result of a plan, of a concerted and well-thought-out invasion of their land. If there was indeed a plan, that would undermine the whole public order and the official explanation of what is happening, the nonsense of the "hate laws" that prevent people from speaking the truth about these events. Following this pattern, people basically learn very little about why these incidents are happening. Nothing can be learned without facing two facts that the liberal ideology of the West in particular chooses not to include.

The first is that the West insists on seeing Islam through the lenses of its own modern, liberal theories about religion, freedom, and human motivation. Islam is just another religion; we are told that it acts like other religions, even when it does not. (The alternate corollary of this view in much Western thought is that all other religions, especially Christianity, are composed of fanatics, just like Islam. In this view all religions are equally bad.) Few will grasp that a singular purpose can be pursued in Islam—and in fact has been pursued for centuries. Such Western theories have their own presuppositions and limitations that make it almost impossible for those who believe them to see clearly what is happening. When the so-called terrorists frankly explain what they are doing—namely, following what it says in their book —they are ignored because, while the explanation fits with the terrorists' understanding of reality, it does not fit with what most people in the West insist on holding.

The second element is that Westerners cannot comprehend that the Qur'an, in the eyes of many Muslims, means just what it says. It is a religion that continually seeks, whether it be gradually or quickly, to conquer the world for Allah by whatever means are at hand in a given century or a given place. Islam does not disdain gradualism if it works, as it often does. Today, we are witnessing not something new but something being renewed in the light of a shrewd estimation by many Muslim thinkers and activists about the weakness and lack of insight on the part of those who might naturally be expected to oppose this expansion.

The much-controverted statement of the nineteenth-century British prime minister William Gladstone (1809–1898) that we will have violence from Islam as long as the Qur'an is read seems very close to the truth, both of the historical record and of the text itself. Many want to sanitize the text by eliminating or reinterpreting the many passages in the Qur'an that insist on this expansion. But to follow this procedure is to change the Qur'an so that it is not the same book that was said to have been revealed to Muhammad. We have to say either that the Qur'an does not say what it says or that it does not, contrary to centuries of faithful readers, mean what it says. The third alternative is to look at what many Muslims in fact did do in the light of this history: they accepted a theory of voluntarism that allows the changing of words and ideas at will, so that there is no set intelligence in any revealed word.

President Trump came as close as any recent political leader in putting his finger on the problem. But even he did not state the fact that we are now witnessing moral aberrations on a regular basis in these sequential bombings. The "aberrations", if we must use that term, are on the side of those who cannot bring themselves to admit the facts, historical and contemporary, that indicate that the problem is within Islam itself—not just with "terrorists" who supposedly have little or nothing to do with Islam. No doubt some recent Muslim intellectuals have dallied with nationalist or Leninist thinking, but they did not need this to justify their efforts to continue the historic Muslim effort to conquer the world for Allah.

The president wants Muslims themselves to identify such

terrorists within their own families and communities and to get them out of their countries. It will never happen. If we read the statistics on the estimated numbers of jihadists already in foreign countries, they already are busy at this task of expanding Islam. This is the source of the continued bombings. The trouble is that such large numbers of young and mostly male Muslims in every Western country are not there simply because they are poor or have been expelled as unwanted from Muslim states. They are there to expand Islam. This is why we have bombings. These young men and their shrewd leaders have judged that the best way to continue this expansion into hitherto-difficult territory is to infiltrate it through a combination of violence and democratic-demographic use of existing laws. The massive invasion of refugees has included many bent on expanding Islam into Europe in particular. We can add the demographic dynamic of frequent birth of Muslim children in contrast to a rapid decline in birth among Europeans.

The Muslim method of expansion begins with a refusal to integrate into any new society. They set up their own enclaves and quickly establish their own internal laws and enforcements. The purpose of Muslim expansion is not to assimilate into a new nation and culture but rather to change it so that it conforms to Muslim ways. This keeping apart does not mean that the laws and customs of other lands cannot be used for purposes of the expansion of Islam. No classic Western laws have aided Muslim expansion more than those that guarantee freedom of speech and religion, as well as those fostering diversity in a manner that makes judging the real direction of Islamic presence almost impossible.

III

The expansion of Islam into at least the Western world is, as far as I can see, going quite well. Its would-be opponents (and victims) are confused by what it is and by their own ideological explanations of reality, particularly religious reality. This latter confusion could not be a more welcome thing for those Muslim thinkers and actors who are engaged in promoting this widespread expansion of Islam into areas of the world where it has not been previously found. India, of course, is the one country that is now formed by the refusal of its former northern Muslim provinces to stay in India. India has one of the largest Muslim populations in the world, though Muslims in that country are still a minority. Muslim-Hindu struggles go back centuries. Muslim forces now regularly test the Philippine southern islands. China, Japan, Korea, and Vietnam are largely future projects for Islam. Malaysia and Indonesia are Muslim nations. Islam is active and successful in Africa. It has footholds in North America and looks carefully at Latin America. Within all Muslim nations themselves we also find a struggle between a status quo establishment and the newly energized movements to return to the jihad, to the expansion of Islam.

The Saudis have been busy financing the construction of thousands of mosques and promoting other pro-Muslim academic and social entities all over Europe and the Americas. Many Christian churches have been torn down in Muslim lands. They have been closed or abandoned in Europe and America due to the decline in the number of believers; Muslims would like to take possession of some of these abandoned edifices. Mosques are now found almost everywhere in the world. They are not simply built by local money or members. They are clearly part of a plan. We are witnessing one of the most remarkable expansions of concrete Islamic presence in centuries. Meanwhile, the project of ridding the Muslim lands in the Middle East of Christian presence has been almost completed, creating many known and unknown Christian martyrs. This attack on Christians has been, with few exceptions, little more than noted. There has been little effort to insist that the freedom provided Muslims in Western countries be reciprocated in Muslim lands; when such efforts have been made, the success has been minimal. Until this demand is made a central element in Western thinking and policy, no Muslim government will worry too much about it.

Is there anything that might stop this dynamic Muslim expansion? Islamic thinkers recognize that, at bottom, much of the West is governed in principle by the same voluntarist philosophy that Islam has accepted to justify its own incoherence. The only thing voluntarist systems recognize as binding is force. But force is relatively useless until it is seen within a system that knows how and where to use it. Islamic leaders have every right to think that they can greatly extend the boundaries of Islam into Europe in the near future by using the democratic process made available to them in these lands. What it would take to deter expansion is an effort that would itself not depend on relativist or liberal ideas about religion. Yet Christianity seems itself to be no longer exempt from these same relativist tendencies to provide any effective counterforce.

Still, what makes Islam vulnerable is what it says and believes about itself. It believes that the Qur'an is the final revelation of Allah, and it does not hold itself to be bound by natural justice. These are very dubious premises. These are the two weakest tenets of the religion and the ones most in need of attention in dealing with Islam. The Qur'an is said to originate directly from Allah. It claims to be the final revelation that corrects earlier revelations (Old and New Testaments). It specifically denies the Trinity, the Incarnation, the Cross, and the Resurrection. If the Qur'an is true, Christianity cannot be true. The Qur'an is said to have no human origin or input. Since this belief governs the thinking in Islam, a valid and critical edition of the Qur'an is needed. Though much reflection is found on the words and ideas of the Qur'an, it is astonishing that no critical edition exists either in the West or in Islam.

For some time now, a group of German scholars has been working on the *Corpus Coranicum*. This endeavor seeks to locate and publish all the earliest texts of the Qur'an, together with commentaries. The Qur'an contains within itself sources that are older than Islam: writings from the Old Testament and the apocryphal gospels. The earliest texts of the Qur'an do not appear until a century after Muhammad. Insofar as this critical edition suggests that the Qur'an is not what it claims to be, its publication will be slow (some give the date of 2025) and dangerous, if it appears at all. Fear of retaliation is always present in dealing with a critical edition that finds anything suspicious in the origins of the Qur'an.

The belief that Islam has nothing to do with violence must be confronted. This belief cannot be maintained on the basis of Islamic texts or the historical record. The problem of natural justice can be used as a tool to confront the most visible objections to Islam today, namely, the killings of innocent people. Of course, this approach is open to the objection that similar things are done in the West. It just depends on what one objects to. The number of those killed in jihadist-type atrocities is large, but so is the number of those killed by abortion in the West. Islam is far more just on this score than most of the Western countries. What is to be noted is that both justifications—jihad and abortion—rest on voluntarist principles. This means, in essence, that the primary struggle with Islam is also a struggle with ourselves about the grounds of reason.

Both in the case of a critical edition of the Qur'an and in the dealing with arbitrary killings of innocents, we need a common standard of reason. This point, of course, is what Benedict XVI pointed out in his Regensburg lecture. The reaction of some Muslims was one of violence, which proved his point; the Western reaction was one of indifference. But the fact is that the disorders in Islam and in the West have a common origin. Until this source is recognized, the violence in both areas will continue and grow. Or to put it another way, violence as such is not the problem; violence is only the problem's external manifestation. The real issue is that *Deus logos, non voluntas, est.*

24

The Attacks in Barcelona Are Part of a Growing Worldwide War

I

The truck slaughter in Barcelona on August 17 brings up a question that the North Koreans must be pondering. Attacks with trucks receive as much world attention as nuclear weapons; they are also far less expensive. Surely, the ISIS method of getting world attention is much cheaper and more effective than the furious North Korean effort to produce and deliver nuclear weapons on target. Indeed, we see ISIS' hold of its formally controlled areas in Iraq and Syria becoming more and more tenuous. But it does not follow that we will see a corresponding lessening of jihadist activity elsewhere. It may well increase. Ideas and "divine" missions do not always need a safe place to be effective.

The drawback in this comparison with ISIS is that North Korea is overwhelmingly matched. If it decided to use its nuclear devices, that would mean its own destruction. The North Koreans are not daft. They know the potential consequences to themselves. The Muslim jihadists do not care about death. They have the tactical advantage, month after

Adapted from "The Attacks in Barcelona Are Part of a Growing World-Wide War", *Catholic World Report*, August 20, 2017, http://www.catholicworldr eport.com/2017/08/20/the-attacks-in-barcelona-are-part-of-a-growing-world -wide-war/.

month, of actually killing perceived enemies. They are not afraid to die for their cause, while the North Koreans only cautiously threaten.

Besides, Muslim violent incidents can and do happen anywhere in the world at any time. Almost the whole planet is now set up with various screenings and searches to protect from random Muslim jihadists. With massive recent Muslim immigration into Europe and America, however, few places in these areas are really safe. Western law and custom often work to the advantage of the jihadists. A new fear has become the norm in all societies in which citizens were once able to move about in their own cities and towns without worry.

Muslims of all kinds, as noted, are everywhere, while the North Koreans are largely confined to North Korea, an out-of-the-way corner of the world. There are twenty-five million North Koreans, but we count some billion or more Muslims of various origins, persuasions, and sects. North Korea cannot hope to take over the world or make it Korean. It can only disrupt or destroy parts of it to obtain what it wants.

The Muslims have played their cards well. They have already succeeded in significantly expanding into Europe and America, where they quickly establish their own exclusive enclaves. They have mostly reached the goal of eliminating all significant non-Muslim presence from what are claimed to be exclusively Muslim areas in the Middle East. All branches of Islam, moreover, think the world ought to be Muslim. The only controversy, and not a very vigorous one at the moment, concerns what means to use for this purpose: war, numbers, or both—and both are sanctioned by the Qur'an. These means can be used separately or in coordination.

G. K. Chesterton, in his 1933 book on Saint Francis of Assisi, remarked on Saint Francis' failed efforts to convert Muslims in Francis' lifetime (1181–1220). Chesterton added that in Francis' view "it was better to create Christians [by conversion] than to destroy Muslims. If Islam had been converted, the world would have been immeasurably more united and happier; for one thing, three-quarters of the wars of modern history would never have taken place." Francis met the sultan and even seems to have proposed a trial by fire as to the truth of either religion. "Indeed, throwing himself into the fire was hardly more desperate, in any case, than throwing himself among the weapons and tools of torture of a horde of fanatical Mahomedans and asking them to renounce Mahomet."[1] In many cases, to propose that someone renounce his Muslim faith is itself sufficient to cause the death of the person who proposes it.

What interests me in these remarks of Chesterton on Francis of Assisi, however, is the theme of conversion as the only real way of dealing with the long-term issue of Islam. This topic is not wholly unmindful of the famous Donatist heresy in Augustine's time. The central issue then came down to the futility of reasonable efforts to counteract Donatist violence short of forced conversion. Chesterton noted the failure to "build bridges" between these religions and the resulting consequences that separated peoples from one another. The fact is that some positions are incompatible with each other. This fact would seem to result in a pragmatic consequence. Differing but incompatible cultures live separately side by side but rely on some Hobbesian all-powerful state appara-

---

[1] G. K. Chesterton, *St. Thomas Aquinas; St. Francis of Assisi* (San Francisco: Ignatius Press, 2002), 293.

tus that ruthlessly suppresses any manifestations of violence. This view assumes that the state apparatus is not itself in control of the jihadists.

Certainly, in principle, Islam itself sees the solution to the modern project as the conversion of the world to Allah. This aim is a powerful motivation. It inspires millions to take whatever steps are needed to achieve it, including war and terror. Most of the areas that are now Muslim were once populated by Christians. Their conversion was, in one way or another, usually by force or social pressure. It should not surprise us today that the most popular baby boy's name in London is said to be Muhammad. In many ways, from a betting angle based on today's estimates, the conversion of the world to Islam is, in the long run, more likely than its conversion to Christianity. Aside from the Reconquista in Spain and some similar moves in the Balkans, there has been no real success of Christianity to convert Islam. The Crusaders were ultimately defeated. As a result of this seemingly impossible project of converting Islam, several Christian thinkers have developed dubious theories that see the Qur'an and its observance to be "salvific" in Christian terms.

The cause of turmoil coming from Islam cannot, as many suppose, be attributed to poverty, development, politics, nationalism, or any other motivation. The basic cause is a religious belief in the truth of the Muslim mission as set down in the Qur'an. Until that motivation is taken seriously and taken for what it is, we will not understand what is happening, and has been happening since Islam's foundation in the world in the seventh century. Many cannot or will not believe that such abiding motivation over time is possible. They thus propose other causes that must be, so they hold, the "real" cause of Muslim aggression. But in fact, in Islam's own terms the motivation is religious. The aggression can be met only if we begin with that truth. The question then becomes, as it should have been all along, whether this religion is true or not.

Islam presents itself, in spite of its jihadist elements—or perhaps because of them—as a religion of peace. The string of bombings and truck-caused deaths that we have seen in the past decade seems at first to belie this affirmation. The Qur'an itself certainly gives sufficient reason to make every effort to expand Islam, by violent jihad if opportune or necessary. But in most Islamic thought, peace can happen only after the world is converted to Allah. Until that time, the world is divided into areas of peace, that is, areas under Muslim control, and areas of war, that is, everywhere else. Technically, all those not in the sphere of Islam are enemies and at war with Islam. When the suicide bomber kills any enemy, the question of any guilt over a crime against the innocent does not come up. There are no innocent people in the zone of war. So if one is killed while killing enemies, he, not the enemy, is the martyr.

As long as the Qur'an is carefully and authoritatively read and believed by new generations, this expansive mission will be alive in the world. It is forever in the book. If we maintain that the Qur'an is the word of Allah, that it is blasphemous to change it, and if it teaches that all individuals and societies must be ruled by Allah, then we will never rid ourselves of its dynamism until we can show that its sources and practices are not and cannot be valid or true.

In its voluntarist option, Islam has sought to protect itself from the severe criticism that arises from reason, especially against its practical denial of the principle of contradiction. As there are many inaccuracies and contradictions in the Qur'an, Muslim thinkers early on recognized that they faced a serious problem, a problem intrinsic to their dealing with Greek philosophy. As Aquinas noted in the *Summa contra gentiles*, many profound attempts by Averroës and Avicenna in particular were made to deal with the relation between Muslim revelation and reason.

The result in general went with al-Ghazali that the basis of things was not *logos* but *voluntas*. This meant that Allah could say one thing one day and another thing the next. If Allah were limited to reason, it was thought, he would not be all-powerful; he would not be the master of both good and evil. The result of this line of thinking was to place the will of Allah at the center of things, both moral and physical. Every existing thing could at any time be otherwise. The only law was Allah's changeable will. Each thing could be its opposite, if Allah so willed. The only proper attitude to such a god was not to try to make sense of his decrees and demands but to submit to them no matter what they held. Anything less was considered blasphemous and would be punished as such.

III

The formal rejection of any basic element in the Qur'an, like the call for jihad, would imply that we can reject the original text as handed down from Allah. The Qur'an's claim to its own truth demands that its text and teaching remain the same. In Muslim teaching, only Allah can change his teaching, which he has done. That is why contradictory elements are found in the Qur'an. When any change happens, the last change is what counts. The words of the Qur'an come directly from Allah; to undermine either their meaning or their connection with Allah is, in effect, to deny any truth claim that might exist in the Qur'an. This principle is why we cannot change Islam into something else that it is not. It must either be as it is or not at all.

When the Qur'an talks of peace, it does not mean the co-existence of various traditions or religions under one roof. If it has to live under such a varied system, it does so under coercion until such time as it can gain the upper hand by force, or by political or demographic means. Peace means the condition of the world when every part of the world is submissive to Islam. Until that time, Islam is, in one way or another, at war with what is not yet under its authority. We may not like to hear this view. The Muslims may not like to hear it either. The issue, however, is, what does the religion advocate? A loyal believer, one who has no means to appeal to the primacy of reason, will follow what it teaches.

This attitude to be obedient to what the Qur'an says is why we must not hesitate to acknowledge that jihadists and other promoters of the expansion of Islam are in principle pious believers, more so than those who know what the Qur'an says but do not have the courage to pursue it. It is why there is a struggle within Islam itself over its true meaning. The one thing that cannot be done without undermining the very premises of the religion itself, however, is to claim that its text can be "reformed" to eliminate what it says about world conquest.

In conclusion, to return to the theme of conversion, I would argue that, (1) even if the incoherence of voluntarism in Islam can be demonstrated, or (2) even if critically the text of the Qur'an can be shown not to have come directly from the hands of Allah, the only real way to eliminate the historic aggressiveness of Islam is to convert its believers. Of course, in theory, they might be converted to anything.

If Islam cannot or will not be converted to the truth, it is probably best to let it be and do what is possible to deter it.

Islam stands as a judgment on the nations. It also stands as a judgment on thought itself. Once any culture, including our own, abandons as the basis of its legal, political, philosophical, or religious thought the central role of the principle of noncontradiction, almost anything can follow. Islam, ironically, stands as the great teacher of mankind. It teaches it at least one of the things that happen when we keep our faith but reject the guidance of our reason.

25

On the Future of ISIS

What exactly has been defeated in the recent battles against Islamic State, or ISIS? The relative success of ISIS in recent years has been made possible largely by the failure of its opponents to understand what it is. Its military successes in the Near East and the worldwide turmoil it has caused by frequent suicide bombings, truck crashings, and shootings can hardly be unknown anyplace in the world. ISIS is often said to be a "terrorist" organization unrelated to or not identified with Islam. Once it is isolated and neutralized, the theory goes, everything can return to normal.

The current military defeats of ISIS will test this thesis. One school of thought maintains that the threat will now largely disappear. Peaceful Muslims will be in charge in what are called their own lands. The other school thinks that ISIS is now free to pursue a more lethal and worldwide expansion in the vast new areas in which Muslim presence is now being rapidly established. A morally decadent West, in its own areas, will find itself unable to cope with the zeal of

The original version of this essay appeared in *Crisis*, November 2, 2017, http://www.crisismagazine.com/2017/on-the-future-of-isis.

what is, to it, a strange new religion now encamped in its midst.

The Trump administration has been more systematic than that of Obama. It has paid careful military attention to the once-thought triumphant ISIS arms—with its trucks, tommy guns, and black uniforms. Most of its strongholds, now largely in ruins, have been retaken. Millions of locals have fled the area, usually for Europe, but for wherever they could land. A concentrated persecution of Christians and other non-Muslim groups has decimated many of the most famous cities and areas in Iraq, Syria, and Palestine. The White House has just recognized the bias against persecuted Christians when refugee services relied solely on United Nations agencies.

Under a more centered military attack, ISIS leaders were killed or placed under constant threat. Recruits have begun to surrender. These men have been responsible for some of the worst crimes against innocent human beings in history. Their practice of beheading their enemies on TV has left a deep, sickening impression, as it was intended to do. In their own minds, no doubt, ISIS members carried out these atrocities under a religious motivation. Sufficient justification exists in Islamic texts and military traditions for their zeal and methods.

It has been a major failure of intelligence in dealing with ISIS and its affiliates to classify them as members of a group that enjoyed killing for the sake of killing. ISIS fighters conceive themselves as loyal troops doing a work that Allah wills. The mission to convert the world to Allah fires the soul of anyone who takes the Qur'an seriously.

A modern man finds it difficult to believe that a project that began some twelve centuries ago in far-off Arabia could be reinvigorated, could be a constant threat in century after century since then. But many in Islam have no trouble in understanding this abiding mission, which if it is defeated or fails in one era, will reappear in another, inspired by the same sources.

But the defeat of self-proclaimed Muslim arms is not worthless. Islam is a religion that sees itself under the will of Allah. Under this inspiration they are urged to expand the initial mission to submit the world to Allah. If they are set back or stopped by superior military force at a given time or place, a Tours or a Vienna, it is looked upon as a defeat for Allah. Hence, they begin to doubt their mission.

But the thinkers who inspire the expansion of Islam are also hard realists. They know that the migration of millions of Muslims into Europe and America represents an opportunity for them unparalleled in their recent history. They are already on the ground of the nations that they want next to conquer, nations that once blunted their thrusts into Europe. They are often welcomed there and given the privileges of citizenship.

Their new hosts often think that they will be able to attract them to peaceful coexistence with non-Muslims through association with the so-called modern secular world. All Islam needs to do is rid itself of any aspiration to reestablish its own law and customs.

What is happening, however, is the realization that Islam does not assimilate. It recreates its own enclaves, laws, mosques, dress, diet, and familial customs wherever a sufficient number of Muslim people are present. In addition, the birthrate of Muslims is considerably higher than that of secular Europeans. As a result of the ISIS experience, two things became clear to many Muslim thinkers. One is that terror, at least in the short run, works. Even the crashing of a truck into a crowd at a market becomes an international incident. Modern armies, while effective against ISIS in an open field, are not so useful when it comes to preventing the chaos that random attacks against civilians can cause. The defeat of ISIS in the Near East may well result in an increase of Muslim aggression elsewhere.

Regardless, the Islamization of Western cities and countries, by Muslims taking advantage of the laws and the democratic processes of the societies in which they find themselves, is well underway. In the end, we can expect that more and more areas will be subject to the laws and the customs of Islam, now updated through the recent ISIS lessons.

26

What, Indeed, Is the Qur'an?

Most people know that the Qur'an is the holy book of the Muslim religion, hence of about a fifth of the world's population. But knowing this much, we still must grasp the peculiar nature of this famous book, if, indeed, because of its origins, it can be called precisely a "book". If we ask just when this book was written, or even, who exactly wrote it, we soon run into difficult issues.

First, we have to ask: "What do Muslims think the book is?" Then we have to ask: "What does it look like it is considering the empirical and historical analyses of its origins and content?" The effort to understand what the Qur'an is becomes doubly difficult because Muslims themselves will not allow any investigation into or questioning of its original sources if it contradicts what the religion insists that it is, namely, a direct revelation from Allah, the Muslim name for what it calls "God". Any significant divergence from the classic Qur'anic text will be met with the accusation of blasphemy, which can result in serious legal and even penal repercussions.

Originally published in *Crisis*, January 9, 2018, https://www.crisismagazine .com/2018/what-indeed-is-the-quran.

According to the French historian Rémi Brague, two consequences follow from the way Islam considers itself: (1) no religion preceded Islam, which is the religion of Abraham, Noah, and even Adam, therefore Islam has inherited nothing and owes nothing to anyone; and (2) the holy books of the other religions (the Torah, the Gospels) are not the prefigurations of the Qur'an but, on the contrary, distorted versions of an original message that essentially coincides with it.[1] Islamic scholars account for the obvious antiquity of the Old Testament, and the parts of it that were rewritten and included in the Qur'an, by claiming that Allah had written the Qur'an before the writing of the Old Testament began. Indeed, they claim that Allah wrote the Qur'an in his mind before Creation itself. With no evidence to support such claims, however, Muslims have presumed that the Old and New Testaments were mysteriously rewritten by Jews and Christians to exclude Muhammad's name and teachings, which were said to be in the original text from Allah.

A second problem arises because the text of the Qur'an, as we know it, was not written or put together as a single opus until decades after Muhammad's death (A.D. 632). In addition, the organization of the text has no internal logic. It is pasted together according to the length of the passages, not their chronology or meaning. Here is how Samir Khalil Samir, S.J., put the matter:

> Once the official version [of the Qur'an] was published and disseminated, the khalif 'Uthmān [d. A.D. 656] ordered the destruction of all other versions. Hence, the *uthmana* version realized on the khalif's initiative is the Qur'ān we have today. It is the result of compromises between the seven *huffāz*, who often differed one from another. Therefore, it

[1] Rémi Brague, *On the God of the Christians (and on One or Two Others)*, (South Bend, Ind.: St. Augustine's Press, 2013), 128.

is impossible to assert with any degree of certainty that a
particular section of the Qur'āñ is the authentic statement
truly pronounced by Muhammad. The original revelations
were made over a period of eight thousand days between
the years 610 and 632, and no human being could pretend
to have such a perfect memory to recall, after many years,
the exact words heard only once.[2]

In other words, the text of the Qur'an, which is said to have
come directly from Allah through Muhammad, was put together in such a way that it could not be verified. Most of
the original texts on which it was based were destroyed so
that the final text could not be re-examined in the light of
its composition. However, at least some of these cast-away
texts have been located and are under study.

The Qur'an is said to have been written in pure Arabic. Its literal origin, so it is said, was in the mind of Allah who passed it unchanged directly through Muhammad
to mankind. Technically, Muhammad had nothing to do
with the basic content of the Qur'an. That belonged to Allah. Hence, it was considered unchangeable. The book contained Allah's detailed instructions about what to believe and
about how men are to live. It includes promises of the rewards for so doing and the punishments in hell for not following Allah.

But "What sort of a 'book' is the Qur'an?" It turns out
to be something that is not so easily explained. On request,
anyone can obtain a free copy of the Qur'an from several
easily found online Muslim sources in just about any language. It is found in most libraries. It can be purchased on
Amazon or in bookstores. But once we have a copy of the
Qur'an in our hands, what is it that we actually have?

---

[2] Samir Khalil Samir, S.J., *111 Questions on Islam*, (San Francisco: Ignatius
Press, 2008), 45.

Many claim that, if we do not know Arabic, we will not really understand its true meaning. The Qur'an itself says that we have to be properly disposed to read it even in Arabic. If we do not understand it, it is our fault. The book is intended to be the final revelation of Allah to mankind.

As we noted, the Qur'an is said to predate all other scriptures, including the Old and New Testaments, even though it came in time after them. Just how and why this predating is possible constitutes one of the dubious aspects of the claim of the Qur'an to be what it says it is. If Muhammad lived in the seventh century A.D., how on earth could he have known Abraham, Isaac, and David?

If we ask a research scholar, "What is the Bible?", he will give us a long explication of the available sources from which the Bible was fashioned. He will not so much care about what it says or means. He will want to know how it was put together from these fragments and texts that we still possess. The Bible, in this sense, has been and continues to be meticulously worked over so that we know as best we can the authentic "text" of Scripture. This textual work is conceived as supportive of, basic to, a valid reading and understanding of the content of Jewish or Christian revelation.

When it comes to the Qur'an, we run into the fact that it was not put together in its present form until decades after Muhammad's death. There seems to have been many full and partial versions of Muhammad's words floating about the Arabic world in his time. This variety of texts could cause trouble for a revelation that was, in its own wording, final and unchanging. The caliph Uthman, as Samir Khalil Samir pointed out, decided to produce a "definitive" edition. After conflating into one all the texts deemed authentic, he ordered all other copies of the Qur'an to be destroyed.

Evidently, however, some of these earlier versions have

survived in Yemen and other places. A group of German scholars for a number of decades now have struggled, against the bitter opposition of many in Islam, to produce a definitive critical edition of the Qur'an, one that would take into consideration these variant texts. The fact that, up to now, a critical edition of the Qur'an does not exist is something of an academic scandal. But it is understandable when we realize that the very lives of those who come up with any questioning of the validity of the Qur'anic text are threatened.

What is the problem here? Basically, it is this: it may turn out that the text of the Qur'an is little more than a hastily gathered collection of unrelated texts put together after Muhammad's death. This origin would mean that the Qur'an cannot be what it claims to be. Hence, we have the bitter opposition to having the Qur'an examined carefully for its unity or coherence.

But if we look on the Qur'an from the Muslim side, we can more easily see the problem. In the seventh century A.D. there suddenly arose a revelation that maintains it is the last and final revelation of Allah. The book contains dozens of characters and stories that are clearly taken from the Bible, such as Adam, Abraham, Noah, and David, as well as Jesus and Mary. To the normal observer, the Qur'an must have borrowed these people and events from the Jewish and Christian Scriptures. Yet, if this historical origin is shown, then the Qur'an is merely the product of a confused effort to rewrite the Scriptures already in existence.

Unless some thesis can be developed whereby the Jewish and Christian Scriptures are wrong, and therefore in need of revision, we have no reason to give any credence to the Qur'an. Besides, Muhammad is nowhere to be found in either the Old or the New Testament. The explanation for his absence is that he was later excised by Jews and Christians from their Scriptures. Muslims claim, however, that the Qur'an is not only older than Abraham and Adam, but older than the world itself. It was as it now exists already in the mind of Allah. The Qur'an thus is a rewrite of the Scriptures to clarify what they originally said. There is, of course, no textural or archeological evidence that anything like this rewriting ever happened. But since the claim is fundamental to Islamic convictions about the Qur'an, it must be defended in a way that allows no examination or opposition.

Another basic problem with the Qur'an has been implicitly granted by Muslim scholarship and tradition. Many basic passages in the Qur'an contradict each other. At one time Allah says this, at another he says the opposite. Normally this contradiction would be enough to discredit the whole enterprise. But the belief that Allah could contradict himself developed intellectually and historically in Islam. Will (voluntarism) not reason came to be accepted as the basis of everything. If Allah were not able to contradict himself, it was decided, he would not be all-powerful. We would blaspheme if we denied him this absolute power.

If in the Qur'an one thing is right, say jihad, in one time but not in another, what are we to believe? The Muslim thinkers developed a theory that the last statement in time was the one that was binding. In the Qur'an the pious Muhammad that appeared early in Mecca is quite different from the warrior Muhammad who later appeared in Medina. It was from the Medina Muhammad that the wars of Islam against the rest of the world originated. But the wars of Islam are not just wars.

One of the remarkable things about Islam, of course, is its holding itself steady over time to the mission that Allah gave his followers—namely, to submit the world to Allah and his law. Islam is still true to this universal mission. If we cannot believe that this abiding purpose over time is possible or indeed in effect, we cannot understand the history of the world as it has faced Islam since Muhammad sent out troops from Medina.

The Qur'an cannot be changed or "reinterpreted" and remain what it is. Wherever its text is read, it will inflame not a few souls, usually young men, to take up the mission of subjecting the world to Allah. The Qur'an is not just a book to read. It is a book that sends men into the world with a flaming purpose. We may have a difficult time understanding this fact, but that is our problem.

The Qur'an is a book that tells of the life and mission of Muhammad, the prophet. The book specifically denies that Christ was the Son of God or that there is otherness in the Godhead. Yahweh and Allah are not the same God. In the Qur'an, Christianity as such is simply rejected as having no validity. It need not be totally suppressed if its members accept second-class citizenship and pay a tax. We may not like to hear this teaching, but no good Muslim, unless he is trying to deceive us, has any doubt that Allah is exactly as he is described in the Qur'an. The Qur'an is a book about man's complete submission to Allah. Islam will gladly overturn the world to make this submission prevail. It will only fail if it is prevented.

Conclusion

This chronology has looked at events from 2006 to 2017 and has offered explanations of these events. I have again and again looked at the reasons given for a "peaceful" Islam and for one that is aggressive and intent on world order under the aegis of Allah. If there is any overriding view that I have had throughout this decade, it has been that of realism. I have thought that the understanding of Islam begins primarily with its history, its book, and its philosophy that explains why so many contradictory things can be accepted almost without a murmur. I have appreciated the use of force both as an instrument of conquest in Islamic history and as a legitimate defense for those who have to confront such force.

Yet, I am in agreement with the famous view that "ideas have consequences." I think that both the strength and the weakness of Islam lie in the order of thought. Within Islam, it seems to me that those who advocate and follow the jihad as a way finally to achieve what Islam has long sought have the better side of the argument. And if the only basis we accept for understanding such a view is voluntarism, then the right and might correspond. If there is, however, a real *logos*, a reason, in the Divinity, in our souls, and in things, then we must confront the expansion of Islam in another way. We must see, as I said earlier, its "fragility"—its relation, or lack of it, to science and reason—as the avenue we must take in understanding what Islam is.

Islam is a religion. It does advocate violence in the achievement of its lofty goal. But at bottom, it cannot explain the real origins of its own Qur'anic texts and justify its treatment of "infidels" as anything but aggressors. Calling everyone outside the inner zone of Muslim peace to be enemies, subject to death, is simply wrong, as is the second-class status of all non-Muslim people within the religion's present orbit.

I recognize the validity of efforts to render Muslims less violent by having them declare loyalty to the nation and not exclusively to the religion. But this approach is valid only if the nation itself does not become another voluntarist ideology based on a theory of "rights" that dissolves all human bonds. Apologists for Islam are right to see much moral decadence in non-Muslim countries. They are slower to see the moral difficulties in the way women, families, and dissenters are treated in their own order. In the end, I am under no illusion. I think it very possible, if not likely, that Islam will successfully establish itself in many areas of Europe and America. It will very likely spread further south in Africa. Even Russia and China are concerned, as are India and the Philippines.

Since this is a chronology of a certain period, I anticipate the next event: a bombing in Berlin, in the Vatican, in Manila, in Stockholm, or in some other venue of high profile. At present, even with changing Western regimes, any prospect seems lacking of a coherent facing of the overall moral, political, and religious problems that the existence of Islam causes in the world, both to itself and to others. The numbers of invaders into Europe will continue. Islam today understands both the value of winning by democratic means and winning by military means. For the most part, those who oppose Muslims do not understand the religious zeal that motivates this expansion.

Islam is strong, very strong. I cannot see how the religious nature of Islam is coherent; yet it is easy to see that it is a fact. The conclusion that I would draw from these ongoing commentaries is: We must begin to ask the question of truth both of ourselves and of Islam. Is Islam true or not? We cannot ask this question if we think that no truth as such exists. If we think truth does not exist, we are left with only power, in which whoever wins is the stronger. Necessary truths include the revelation that Islam explicitly denies, the truth of the Trinity and the Incarnation. If it is merely a question of whose will is the strongest, the future of Islam is, I think, quite bright.

Afterword

The chapters of this book are each occasioned by an on-going and well-publicized incident that involves death, religion, and politics, along with the efforts of the author to explain it. During the period in which these pieces appeared, 2002–2017, the following Schall commentaries on Islamic issues, not included in this book, were also published:

"Hilaire Belloc: 'Islam Will Not Be the Loser'", *Catholic Dossier*, 8 (January/February 2002), 8–14.

"On the Term 'Islamo-Fascism'", *Ignatius Insight*, August 15, 2006. This essay is also found in James V. Schall, *The Regensburg Lecture* (South Bend, In.: St. Augustine's Press 2007), 149–60.

"On Taking Islam Seriously", *Crisis*, July 23, 2014.

"What Is Islam Revisited," *Catholic World Report*, January 9, 2015.

"On Blasphemy", *Catholic Thing*, February 3, 2015.

"On Thinking about Islam," *Crisis*, July 27, 2015.

"The True Islam", *Catholic World Report*, January 24, 2016.

"Islam and French Politics", *Homiletic and Pastoral Review*, August 14, 2016.

"Islam and the London Killings," *Catholic World Report*, March 28, 2017.

Bibliography

Ali, Daniel, and Robert Spencer. *Inside Islam: A Guide for Catholics; 100 Questions and Answers*. West Chester, Pa.: Ascension, 2003.

Ansari, Zafar Ishaq, and John Esposito, eds. *Muslims and the West: Encounter and Dialogue*. Washington, D.C.: Georgetown University, 2002.

Aslan, Reza. *No God but God: The Origins, Evolution, and Future of Islam*. New York: Random House, 2006.

Belloc, Hilaire. *The Crusades*. Milwaukee: Bruce, 1937.

———. *The Great Heresies*. New York: Sheed and Ward, 1938.

Bostom, Andrew C., ed. *The Legacy of Jihad: Islamic Holy War and the Fate of Non-Muslims*. Amherst, N.Y.: Prometheus Books, 2005.

Brague, Rémi. *On the God of the Christians (and on One or Two Others)*. South Bend, Ind.: St. Augustine's, 2013.

Caner, Ergun Mehmet. *Unveiling Islam*. Grand Rapids, Mich.: Kregel, 2002.

Charles, J. Daryl. *Between Pacifism and Jihad: Just War and Christian Tradition*. Downers Grove, Ill.: InterVarsity, 2005.

Cooper, Barry. *New Political Religions; or, An Analysis of Modern Terrorism*. Columbia: University of Missouri Press, 2004.

Coren, Michael. *Hatred: Islam's War on Christianity.* Toronto, Ont.: McClelland and Stewart, 2014.

Coughlin, Stephen. *Catastrophic Failures.* Columbia, S.C.: Center for Security Policy Press, 2015.

Esposito, John. *Unholy War: Terror in the Name of Islam.* New York: Oxford, 2002.

Gabriel, Mark. *Islam and Terrorism.* Lake Mary, Fla.: Charisma House, 2002.

Hanley, Matthew. "Aquinas on Islam". *Catholic Thing*, July 28, 2012.

———. "Islam's Inexorable Impulse". *Catholic Thing*, July 7, 2016.

Jomier, Jacques. *The Bible and the Qur'an.* San Francisco: Ignatius Press, 2002.

Kilpatrick, William. "Catholics on Muslim Immigration". *Crisis Magazine*, January 2017.

———. *Christianity, Islam, and Atheism.* San Francisco: Ignatius Press, 2012.

———. "Our Responsibility to Criticize Islam". *Catholic Thing*, December 28, 2016.

———. "Sacrificing the Faith vs. Sacrificing the Faith". *Crisis Magazine*, December 6, 2016.

Ledeen, Michael. *The War against the Terror Masters.* New York: St. Martin's, 2002.

Madden, Thomas. *A Concise History of the Crusades.* Lanham, Md.: Rowman and Littlefield, 2013.

Marlin, George. *Christian Persecutions in the Middle East: A 21st Century Tragedy.* South Bend, Ind.: St. Augustine's, 2015.

Marshall, Paul. *Their Blood Cries Out*. New York: World, 1997.

Mitchell, Joshua. *Tocqueville in Arabia*. Chicago: University of Chicago Press, 2013.

Murawiec, Laurent. *The Mind of Jihad*. Washington, D.C.: Hudson Institute, 2005.

Nasry, Wafik. *The Caliph al-Mahdi and the Patriarch Timothy I: An 8th Century Interreligious Dialogue*. San Bernardino, Calif., 2015.

———. *The Call to Islam and the Birth of the Muslim Brotherhood*. San Bernardino, Calif., 2015.

Norval, Morgan. *The Fifteen Century War: Islam's Violent Heritage*. Indian Wells, Calif.: McKenna, 2002.

Patai, Raphael. *The Arab Mind*. Tucson: Recovery Sources, 2007.

Phares, Walid. *Future Jihad: Terrorist Strategies against America*. New York: St. Martin's, 2014.

Reilly, Robert. *The Closing of the Muslim Mind*. Wilmington: ISI Books, 2011.

Royal, Robert. *The Catholic Martyrs of the Twentieth Century*. New York: Crossroads, 2000.

Samir, Samir Khalil. *111 Questions on Islam: Samir Khalil Samir, S.J., on Islam and the West*. A series of interviews conducted by Giorgio Paolucci and Camille Eid. Edited and translated by Wafik Nasry. San Francisco: Ignatius Press, 2008.

Schall, James V. *The Regensburg Lecture*. South Bend, Ind.: St. Augustine's, 2007.

Scruton, Roger. *The West and the Rest: Globalization and the Terrorist Threat*. Wilmington: ISI Books, 2002.

Spencer, Robert. *Did Muhammad Exist? An Inquiry into Islam's Obscure Origins*. Wilmington: ISI Books, 2012.

————. *The Truth about Muhammad: Founder of the World's Most Intolerant Religion*. Washington, D.C.: Regnery, 2006.

Ye'or, Bat. *Eurabia: The Euro-Arab Axis*. Madison, N.J.: Fairleigh Dickinson University Press, 2005.

Index